The Curmudgeonly Commuter:
"It's all downhill from Edinburgh"

by Graham Dow

Acknowledgements

There are so many people who I need to thank for their support whilst I've embarked on this journey, people who have feigned interest in my stories of this "helping to fill a creative void in my life". You know who you are.

Certain people however, deserve special recognition:

Gary Corcoran: who offered invaluable advice early into this project. In testimony to him, his nickname Corks became an oblique inspiration for the name of a main character.

Beth Paterson: for her ever so gentle but direct assessment of the fourth draft of the book. (There were six drafts in the end).

Neil McPherson: one of my favourite people, a great man, whose varied reactions to many situations became an inspiration.

Keith Stevens: The original curmudgeon on BowieNet.

Ruth Johnson: an amazing lady who offered me her invaluable support and understanding over many months, helping me to stay focused and motivated on this project amongst many others.

Valerie McLeod: who diligently scoured the book for flagrant misuse of hyphens, commas and apostrophes. (Apparently this is something for which I have a natural talent, given it happened on virtually every page).

Tom Blakesley at Twentythree04 Design (www.2304.co.uk): for designing the cover of the book.

The more discerning amongst you will notice littered throughout the book, references to a particular artist who was my own guiding light for what feels like my whole life. He was my colour television in a world of radios and his music and art taught me to be brave, to be bold and to believe that it's entirely fine to think differently. His personal light sadly diminished on 10th January 2016, but the world has kept turning since (something which has come as a pleasant surprise).

Most of all and above everyone else, my wife Jacqueline and my daughter Emily remain my biggest inspirations and critics, and their support is something I'll never truly be able to acknowledge in a way which does it justice. Thank you both so much just for being here, and there, for me. This book is dedicated to you both.

Foreword

This is a book of fiction. The main characters are not based around or about any one individual, particularly not me.

The situations described are of course a combination of my own experiences but also my observations of other people, other people's observations, other people's observations of other people's behaviour - you get the drift. Of course in here are also the many stories which have been passed amongst business travellers for whom the boredom and monotony of travel becomes a central tenet of most conversations.

As an attempt at humour and keeping you mildly entertained, certain situations are naturally exaggerated and possibly even embellished. This is not meant to offend anyone - instead, I'm trying to keep you interested and maybe even laugh at yourself where appropriate.

To try to create character depth, I've also attempted to introduce different human aspects purely in an attempt to offer a more 360 degree experience and view of them. Again, this is entirely fictional and should not be viewed as a commentary on any particular individual.

My intent is to reach out to my fellow business travellers, to entertain them, to acknowledge their pain, frustrations and perhaps even their own prejudices. And of course, to formally record that the life they lead is not, as the uninitiated would imply, "the life"!

This book is the start of a journey for me and I hope to be able to share with you more stories from the developing stable of characters as they grow and sometimes implode.

I would love to hear any comments and observations of your own at curmudgeonlycommuter@gmail.com and of course, reviews are very welcome in the usual places on the web.

Enjoy the read.

Graham Dow
Edinburgh
May 2017

INTRODUCTION

PART ONE
Up The Hill Backwards

PART TWO
The London Boys

INTRODUCTION

Chapter 1
Day In, Day Out

Jamie Sylvester has a nice life.

That's to say, it's fairly normal. He's not bored with what he's doing but similarly, he's not overly excited by it either.

Like most people, the dreams and aspirations he had when he was younger were significantly different to what ended up being his life. In those days, he had a glamorous vision borne from hours spent watching fanciful movies - he was going to be the player, the leader, the Captain of Industry. He saw his future as being free of any financial burden and he wanted to be in complete control of his own destiny.

He's still waiting on his future to arrive though. He doesn't remember ever losing these ambitions and he would go as far to say that they probably still exist. But life sort of overtook him and in reality, it's been ages since he specifically thought about what he wanted to do with his career and his life. He couldn't categorically say he was unhappy, because he's not. It's just this isn't how he thought things would end up - he feels a bit unfulfilled.

Here he is, doing a fairly standard job for a big company in the middle of Edinburgh which doesn't particularly stretch him. It pays well enough - pays better than most if the truth be told - the people are good and everything about it and his life is fairly straightforward.

Nothing really exciting ever seems to happen in his life. Today's morning routine follows a largely predictable course of events.

His alarm has gone off at 0645 at which point, he lies in bed for 15 minutes reading a variety of news websites on his phone.

Then, after a stretch and a ridiculous sounding yawn, he slowly gets up and wanders through to the kitchen to put on the television which merely reconfirms everything he's just read on his phone.

His first of the many coffees he'll have over the next 12 hours, is made in seconds these days courtesy of a machine recommended by George Clooney himself no less, which comes with a variety of little pods. Jamie makes absolutely no effort to work out the different flavours no matter how passionate the people in the store are at selling them. To him, they're a perfectly packaged high dose shot of caffeine and the stronger the better. The colour on the side makes absolutely no difference to his taste buds, although his superstitious nature ensures that the only real thought going into this process is to ensure that no two consecutive selections are coloured the same. He calls it his "little game of coloured coffee rainbow bingo". (Nobody ever laughs when he says that, probably because it's not really that funny).

He's staring aimlessly at the TV now, flicking between the various channels, BBC, Sky News, Good Morning Britain, Sky Sports News, trying at all costs to avoid the commercial breaks whilst keeping one eye on the clock in the corner to make sure he's roughly on time. He pays a bit more attention to the weather, partly because he needs to know whether he'll need an overcoat and partly because he wants to study what the weather girl is wearing today. (When it's the "stand-in bloke" his start to the day can suffer).

Jamie doesn't do stress though. After 20 minutes or so, he wanders off to the bathroom and gazes into the shaving mirror, surveying every new line on his face. He's only approaching thirty but already, there are visible signs of the wear and tear he's put himself through both at university and the intervening years of office life.

He hates the whole process of shaving. The first burst of water splashing on his face which is invariably at a temperature either way too hot or way too cold, followed by the foaming of his light stubble to then feel as if each hair is being pulled out of his face individually using the latest Gillette gadgetry. The stinging of his face afterwards made worse when he applies the ironically marketed "soothing gel".

Cleaning his teeth is far more therapeutic with each tooth being carefully polished with his electric toothbrush buzzing away (assuming it's fully charged of course …) rinsing out the taste of that first morning coffee from his mouth, followed by a routine of flossing. 30 rinses in one direction, and for some reason, only 29 in the other. He doesn't know why, it's just his little way.

The shower has been running in the background for the last five minutes whilst this daily ritual is carried out. Jamie loves his shower and takes in with him an array of bottles each offering a variety of experiences promising to invigorate, soothe, smooth or cleanse. There are more smells rushing out of that shower cubicle than an Arabian spice market.

BANG! BANG! BANG! BANG!

"Jamie!! Will you get a bloody move on!!! Stop bloody preening yourself like some peacock! You don't impress anyone you know" comes a shriek from the hallway.

"Sorry sweets - just be a minute!" shouts Jamie apologetically. Cara, his girlfriend, who up until this point today he has remained largely oblivious to, has a morning routine that no man should ever get in the way of. Jamie did once and regretted it for days. His testicles still flinch at the thought of those 110mm heeled Louboutin shoes!

He skips quickly through to the bedroom still half dripping wet with only a towel around him. He now has his biggest decision of the day (so far) in front of him. Blue suit and patterned tie or grey suit and striped tie? And then there's the shirt - white or blue?

"What did I wear yesterday again? he mutters under his breath.

This really plays with his head. He decides to never again buy blue shirts to reduce at least one decision in the early hours of the day.

Jamie's a bit of a traditionalist and although wearing a suit to work makes him stand out (rather than adopting the alternative work uniform of jeans, a polo shirt and brown shoes) he still prefers to look and be smart. For him, it sets a standard of how he wants to be and be seen and with that, wearing a suit and a tie is something that he chooses to stick to religiously.

By now he's beginning to contemplate the first meetings of the day. He's been doing the same job for roughly three years and it's monotonous to the point that he feels he could do it with his eyes shut. It doesn't excite him anymore (if it ever did) and he's starting to wonder whether it really carries any level of fulfilment for him.

Jamie stares into the full length mirror in his bedroom. He's just short of six foot tall, still relatively athletic in stature and carries himself pretty well even if he says so himself. His hair isn't showing any signs of thinning or receding and it's always neatly groomed with a healthy dollop of the latest pomade.

"Right you are. Ready. Bye Cara - see you tonight sweets!" he shouts as he heads to the front door, not even waiting to hear whether a reply is coming back.

Jamie's regular bus comes at precisely 0758 although it does sometimes come late, maybe as much as three minutes some days, a delay which will determine whether or not he gets his favourite seat by the rear wheel, where it's usually warmer in the winter months. Late buses are unacceptable to Jamie - he'll end up having to stand for most of the twenty minute journey if it runs late and that to him is not why he shells out £1.60 each way.

"What's the point of a timetable if the bus can't keep to it just a bit?" he would moan. His mind races through the multiple implications of this potential late running - everything in his day gets knocked out of sync as a result.

From time to time, he'll acknowledge the drudgery of his routine. He doesn't have too much to complain about per se - it's just that he also doesn't have that much which he can reflect on and feel that proud about. Is this really what he was wanting from his life? True, he gets plenty of time in the evenings to do what he really wants to do, spending time with Cara, watching old films, listening to music or chilling but …

This daily twenty minute period of introspection is as deep as he gets though as he continues to drift through his life.

Occasionally he'll come across other little triggers that grate on him. Triggers which spark at least some signs of emotion and passion within Jamie, signs that say he might have it within him to progress. His life and career that is.

He reckons he has so much more to offer and his early years of ambition haven't produced the outcome he hoped for all those years ago. He wants to be out there making a name for himself. He wants to be flying off to all corners of the world (or even just the UK), cutting deals, leading projects, building things, having strategic dinners in the top Michelin starred restaurants and staying in plush hotels.

He sees some of the company sales guys or, as seems to be the modern description of them Relationship Managers, in the office always carrying around their small travel suitcases, hands stuffed full with receipts from their dinners and hotel stays.

"All they seem to do is smile and have some chat - what do they actually contribute to the place?" he would moan to Cara in the evenings. "These guys are just all front and have no depth at all."

These feelings tended to surface more prominently whenever he saw the relationship managers with whom his team had to deal. On this particular day, he finds himself walking through the rotating doors at the front of his office building behind one of them, Roops Wardhaugh.

"I could do his job easily. I'm smart. I can do stuff" he'd snort says to himself in a firm parody of Fredo Corleone from one of his favourite films, The Godfather.

"I tell stories all the time, people relate to me and I understand way more about our company than they do. All these "Relationship Managers" (using deliberately sarcastic quotation marks with his fingers) ever seem to do is make promises they never keep and sell things that we haven't built yet! They're a liability! I'd love their job. It must be so easy," he'd say.

Jamie is building up both a hatred and a jealousy for them. His boss Pamela would often tell him that this anger isn't healthy, that he should do something about it if he thinks he could do better.

But the fact it's not being offered to him on a plate, the fact that the company can't see what he sees in himself just makes the whole thing grate even more.

As they go through the doors of the building, he catches up with Roops who seems to be in a bit of a daze, distracted even, dragging behind him his little trolley case. Jamie can't help letting his disdain get the better of him.

"You off on a jolly again Roops? Off to your swanky hotels?? You've got the life haven't you? Don't worry about us lot here, doing all the heavy lifting while you're tucking into your next five course dinner!!"

Jamie offers Roops a big slap on the back replacing the sting of his comments with a sting across his upper shoulders.

Roops's eyes just stared at Jamie. He'd heard what was said. He'd heard it a thousand times before. It was a bit boring by now and he could barely muster up the energy to respond. What could he say after all?

"You've got the life, haven't you? Off on another jolly are we?" Those words bore straight through Roops as he stood staring at Jamie.

Once upon a time Roops would have had a well rehearsed reply, laced with a cutting rapier wit. But today was a bad day and he just shrugged.

"Do I really Jamie?" said Roops. "Do I really have "the life"? Is this what "the life" feels like? You haven't got a fucking clue sunshine."

Chapter 2
Cracked Actor

Rupert X Wardhaugh, to give him his full and proper company name, had worked in the establishment for almost 25 years and as such had become a bit of an institution. "Institution" in this sense meaning someone who had survived more restructures than a Labour Party shadow cabinet.

He was obviously valued by the various key decision makers that had been part of the organisation over the years. He wasn't particularly flamboyant in his approach to work being the archetypal "safe pair of hands" but he knew his way about, worked hard, understood his market and most importantly, delivered results year after year.

The strange quirk of the company internal email system bestowed upon him a middle initial - something even his parents hadn't deemed important. To differentiate him from presumably every other Rupert Wardhaugh in the world, and of course within his own organisation, it had been decided that he should be given the letter "X" as a middle initial. Weird.

But despite having one of the most unique names (certainly in the modern world), he was very rarely ever called by his full name, this being an office full of people who had grown up playing semi-professional or amateur football. Wherever this dynamic exists, it comes with an in-built desire to change everyone's name by adding either an "ie" or a "y" to the end of it, meaning "Jones" would became "Jonesy", "Woods" would became "Woodsy" and so on. (For those who studied this closely, it was never clear when names should adopt an "ie" or a "y" at the end - a mystery which one day will surely merit a whole documentary on the Discovery channel in much the same style as say, Stonehenge).

Occasionally, adding an "ie" or a "y" to the end of a name didn't quite sit right notably for example, with Rupert. Had traditional wisdom been followed, it would have resulted in people shouting what sounded like a stage in life when hair starts to sprout from the most intimate parts of your body whenever they wanted to grab his attention.

"Ruperty! You fancy a coffee?" just wouldn't work.

To avoid such embarrassment, an alternative naming convention was introduced which resulted in the shortening of his name - meaning in this instance, Rupert became Roops.

Roops couldn't say with any conviction that he embraced the nickname however it was something he'd lived with for years and it did at least differentiate him. Nobody ever needed to ask "Which Roops?" because there was only one. And he had the bloody letter X in the middle of it just to make sure!

Having been in the company for 25 years, Roops was generally well respected and could get away with perhaps appearing less dynamic than he once was. It wasn't fatigue or a lack of respect - it was a recognition that he'd seen a lot over the years. He could still be slightly pointed in his communications but at least he still had a sense of fun which some took as mischievous but which sometimes others saw as rude or flippant.

Either way, he'd been around long enough to earn himself some level of respect which he didn't think was being offered from bloody Jamie Sylvester. He'd been watching Jamie from a distance with a developing sense of disappointment since he started in the office a few years ago.

In the early days, he saw Jamie as being quite talented but a couple of years of an easy office life meant he'd become lazy.

When things weren't quite being laid to him on a plate, he would complain. He'd forgotten how to stand out from the crowd and this had battered some of that early promise out of him.

He could have been so much more but didn't think or know how to manage himself properly. Winding up senior staff certainly wasn't going to get him seen in a positive light!

Roops headed off to the corner of the office trying to ignore what Jamie had said to him but it was a low day for him and he needed to sit and rationalise it somehow. Those two phrases played over and over in his head, festering and burrowing deep into his conscience.

"You've got the life and off on another jolly? Fuck right off!" he kept saying to himself.

"Is that what people really think goes on? Do they really believe that this company pays people to go off on jollies?" Roops wondered in complete exasperation. "Surely people don't believe that's what still goes on? And of course, that little tit Jamie probably thinks he can do it a whole lot better!"

Roops could never really get used to these comments being thrown at him no matter how often he'd heard them. They would just completely exasperate him.

Comments which would demonstrate a complete lack of understanding around what it means to be a regular business traveller, what he does for a living and the contribution he makes to the company. Comments which definitely didn't even begin to comprehend the real impact – physical and mental – business travel has on the unfortunate souls for whom it is a way of life.

Jamie Sylvester worries about his bus being late but it's highly unlikely that it would ruin his whole day. For Roops, getting to his job could be a complete nightmare even without any delays! He certainly didn't have the luxury of sauntering around in fluffy cotton slippers, coffee in hand, watching early morning news and presumably, the weather girls!

Roops sat there thinking about it all. Seething about it all.

For him, he knows that there is nothing remotely glamorous about getting up at 4am, in the spare room of a house which is mortgaged to the hilt, stumbling around to get showered and then dressing really quietly so as not to waken anyone.

To then get into a taxi driven by a lonely stranger who feels the need to share their life with you. To then stand in a long queue of more complete strangers some of whom you'd believe have had their brains removed before arriving there.

To then be rubbed and breathed on by another complete stranger. To then get on a plane with complete strangers who have lost all control of personal hygiene and insist on invading your personal space.

To then circle the skies over an airport that you'd much rather have landed at 40 minutes earlier.

To then shuffle at snail's pace towards a train – which itself will travel through dark tunnels – which will be full of irritated, short-tempered, defeated looking strangers. To then spend a day having to be nice to people whilst you suffer both sleep deprivation and general frustration - every single week of the year …?

So when the completely uninitiated say "Oh, off travelling again Roops? Get you – living the life aren't you?" he'd want to grab them by the throat and scream "I'm not living the life! It's absolutely fucking shite!! What on earth makes you think sitting inside a metal tube, 25,000 feet in the air, sharing stale farts is in any way at all "the life"?!"

Bumping into Jamie really kicked off his day in a bad way. He hated when people completely undermined what he did and didn't make any effort to think before they spoke.

He thought back to the article he'd once read in an in-flight magazine which had, typically, an article about travelling. In it, they used the quote from Mark Twain who once wrote: "travel is fatal to prejudice, bigotry and narrow-mindedness" which is very true if you're using travel to expand your mind and get new experiences thought Roops. Mark Twain would be one of the people telling Roops that he'd "got the life!"

But that's only half the story. The uninitiated thinks like the holiday traveller who is cradled in the romanticism of discovery, basking in the anticipation of new experiences, of new cultures. The holiday traveller who is satisfying the basic human need and instinct for exploration.

They lay back and dream with a pioneering spirit of breaching new territories, ticking off bucket lists and taking time to relax. They're in no rush with life at that moment – instead they're chilled out with nothing but fresh, crisp white wines, new novels on their electronic gadget thing, an iPod full of tunes and the unmistakeable whiff of excitement at the journey ahead of them.

That, Roops would think, is "the life".

But that's not why he travels. He travels because he needs to. He travels as a means to an end, to get from A to B as quickly and as effortlessly as possible. For Roops, travelling is a purely

19

functional process which more often than not will aggravate and occasionally introduce him to some sort of infection.

"Business travel" he would argue, "is a perfect process ruined consistently by people, weather, poor planning, even poorer processes and well, more people - mostly holidaymakers."

Each component of Roops's day is refined to the minute to allow his main purpose for travelling to function as it's meant to and as soon as one part of the process breaks, which invariably it does, then for him, his whole purpose of travelling is brought into question.

And then of course there is the physical and the mental effort involved in travelling - both on him and those around him. When it doesn't work as it should, then everybody suffers!

So in Roops's mind, there are two types of traveller who can be squarely and oppositely categorised – those who want to travel and those who need to travel. And that difference - adventure versus necessity - introduces lots of opportunity for conflict. When thrown together, as has to happen at airports and train stations, the two don't mix well.

So whilst Mark Twain makes a fair point about the great adventurers and the holidaymakers, he hadn't considered what travelling did for the other half, the business travellers like Roops.

For them, travel is the fuel of prejudice, bigotry and narrow-mindedness. And it's not pretty.

PART ONE
UP THE HILL BACKWARDS

Chapter 3
Wishful Beginnings

Roops lives in a typical suburban part of Edinburgh, well known to most people who live in this fine metropolis. And that that to his mind means that it should be a fairly easy place to find.

He could say this with some confidence because ever since he first came to view the property 10 years ago, he found it easily. Since then, mail and deliveries always arrived without any bother, fast food drivers arrived on time, his friends never mentioned not being able to locate him and once when he checked, even Google Earth had a pretty accurate view of the house's façade.

All of which merely compounded his rage when he asked a professionally qualified person, someone who has allegedly studied for three years to become an expert in their field – which is to connect two addresses in the shortest route and time possible - to get to his house at 5am in the morning and they made such a pig's ear of it.

"You give them one job," he would fume. "One job! It's not like I've asked them to launch a fucking satellite - I only want them to find my house!"

You see, it seems that every day between 4.30am and 6.30am Roops's house disappears. It seems to be wiped from every sat nav, wiped from the memory of every cab driver in Edinburgh and quite simply fails to exist as an entity. It's the modern version of the Bermuda Triangle. Roops and his family now live in some suspended universe hidden from the view of the expertly trained and keen eyed taxi driver.

And of course, all of this is apparently Roops's fault. The blame would appear to sit squarely on his shoulders and his alone.

Now Roops, like most people probably, doesn't particularly enjoy getting up at 4am. For him, who is already something of an insomniac, he has probably had little more than four hours sleep. Despite his protestations that "I can just punch through it" and "Thatcher only needed four hours sleep and she ran a whole country" he really does need more sleep, if only to make him a slightly better human being.

Travelling with four hours sleep just means that every little blockage in his journey becomes an exaggerated nuisance with every lost minute or badly chosen word producing an internal combustion of Vesuvian proportions.

Roops travels with an expectation that he pays for experts to get him from A to B in an efficient, timely and hopefully pleasant manner. He sees it as a contract of sorts – for the exchange of an agreed price he expects to arrive at his destination at roughly the time they agreed at the outset.

"When you meet a friend for a drink, you never say to them 'I'll be there by roughly, er, Tuesday'. You just wouldn't do that so it's even worse when you're actually paying for a service. You have an expectation of at least some professionalism and accuracy," he would moan.

Roops took this all very, very seriously mainly because he needs everyone in his travel plan to meet their promises and their commitments. That way, he can plan his entire day and trip to its maximum effect.

Each part of the process needs to play its part. But when the very start of the entire trip fails because some imbecilic moron can't even find his house (again) it would test even the most patient person - especially on four hours sleep. "No wonder Thatcher took on the miners" he thought, "it was probably because her taxi got lost and put her in a furious mood for the day."

In desperation to try and overcome this issue, Roops recently resorted to giving the taxi company ever more precise instructions for finding his house by trying to remove as much doubt as possible. It seemed that the normal way of doing this, ie by using what he thought was the deft trick of using street names, other house numbers and key landmarks such as trees and ornamental signs was too much for them. If anything, it seemed to confuse them even more.

So he realised he had to be more inventive. He thought about setting off a flare, lighting a beacon on top of his roof or sounding a foghorn but these were all considered to be too dangerous or unneighbourly at such an early time of the day.

Eventually, he resorted to standing at the end of his driveway flashing the torch on his iPhone. This seemed to be the most successful method although for some small pleasure, he did imagine that if the intermittent flashing represented Morse Code, it would probably be spelling out "You must have a tiny knob!".

"If only Morse Code could also do sarcastic tones!" he thought.

With incredible repetition, when the coupling of Roops and his taxi finally happened, he would be met with the same, familiar greeting. It's almost as if every taxi driver in Edinburgh had rehearsed it between them just to wind him up. Roops could mouth it word for word upon stepping into the cab:

"Christ mate, I never knew this place existed …".

And with similarly incredible repetition, Roops would sit and fume whilst struggling to hold together a semblance of politeness. What could he say anymore that was original or didn't come across as rude? It was virtually impossible. Instead, he would just grunt whilst thinking through a variety of the proper responses that he really wanted to give over the years such as:

a) Of course you didn't know it existed. If you had known it existed, you presumably wouldn't have made such an arse of finding it, and me, in the first place?

b) I had already guessed that you didn't know that this place existed because I've just spent the last 20 minutes on the phone guiding you in like a plane landing in thick fog.

c) My finely tuned day, timed to perfection is already 25 minutes behind schedule because not only have you spent 20 minutes finding me, you've now spent another 5 minutes telling me you never knew that my house existed. It's almost as if you still don't believe that right in front of you is an actual house. Apparently, I should have a bigger sign on the garden gate announcing to everyone that I exist or better still, I should move the entire house to a location that you can actually find … which presumably is about a foot from the end of your nose!

This morning Roops slumped in the back of the taxi, quietly seething and praying that today of all days, this would be the trip where he doesn't get a driver who insists on talking to him all the way out to the airport. He had noticed on his many travels that taxi drivers the world over are a breed who appear to be expert in every field possible except perhaps the one thing that they are actually employed to do, namely to find you at an appointed time and take you to your destination quickly and efficiently.

It didn't seem that difficult a thing to do, he thought, aside from the three years of training. It was all a fairly simple arrangement to follow but the whole thing has frustrations and apparently hidden rules which don't seem to be written down anywhere. Maybe they're in the small print somewhere on the back of the fold-up seats.

Over many years of travelling, Roops had honed them down to nine key points:

- Thou shalt listen and engage with me if I choose to impart my considerable knowledge on you
- Thou shalt agree with me at all times especially when discussing politics, football, other cab firms or the local council
- Thou shalt accept that I have absolutely no interest in your views in return
- Thou shalt accept that I always know the quickest route despite all evidence to the contrary
- Thou shalt put up with my huffing and puffing when we hit traffic – even although I'm still getting paid for it and it's you who's going to be late …
- Thou shalt feel guilty for asking to go somewhere that I don't like to go
- Thou shalt also feel guilty for asking to go to Edinburgh Airport because they charge me to get out again
- Thou shalt tip me
- Thou shalt accept my heavily sarcastic tone when the tip isn't big enough

At 5.25am, and with only four hours sleep, Roops is in no mood for conversation, especially with the guy who is responsible for ruining the start of his day in the first place. Roops sat there scowling in an attempt to ward off the driver.

Instead, Roops wanted to sit and fire off multiple emails to everyone he could think off, just to remind them that he was up and they weren't. This "game" being his release from the annoyance of having to be up at 4am with his only company being some buffoon driving a black cab.

It's not that Roops has a chip on his shoulder but he does always think it's useful to let everyone know that even when he's not in the office, he still exists. And more than that, he's also clearly very dedicated.

"And they think my life is all glamour?" he'd think.

The content of the email he writes is almost irrelevant of course – it's the message of the message that's important. It says in a puffed-out-chest sort of way: "Here I am, working already, still thinking, always "on", still relevant."

His emails seeped with anger and self pity.

But today, the emails have to wait because Roops's new best friend, Mr Edinburgh Taxi Driver, ignoring the body language of the tired, barely living carcass in the back, decides to strike up a conversation. Roops' opportunity to feel important to his company is lost for a while at least.

Now remember, Roops is very tired and he needs to save every ounce of good thought for his meetings during the day ahead. This means that he can't afford to spend energy on trying to out-think his taxi driver which puts him at a terrible disadvantage and consequently he becomes easy prey. And this predator needs no second invitation.

"You aff somewhere nice then?" comes the voice from the front.

Roops quickly checks himself up and down, just in case he'd forgotten to change out of his khaki safari suit and pith helmet from the weekend.

Here he is in a dark navy suit, polished brogues, a crisp white shirt and a tie fashioned with a firm and neat Windsor knot. He then glances over to his little hand-luggage sized travel case, stuffed full of similar clothes.

Nothing at all about him looks like he has prepared to go anywhere "nice". When Roops goes somewhere "nice" he never, ever dresses like this.

"Er, no. Just off to London for a few days." comes the strained reply.

"Aw right. Ah've been tae London wance. Ah didnae like it. It wus too big for me an' the missus - loads o' tourists like …"

"Really? There were a lot of tourists?" enquired Roops. "You must have been very unlucky that weekend …"

"Aye, tons o' them. Frae all over the world as well … kept getting under ur feet," says the voice from the front. And then, with absolutely no continuity to the conversation, out of nowhere comes the question Roops dreads.

"So whit do you dae fur yer cumpnay then?"

Oh god … Roops's heart sinks.

It's not actually that simple to explain you see. Even he struggles sometimes to make it sound important because to the lay person, it sounds a bit lame. He could try really hard to give context to the role but he's very tired, a bit irritated at the whole "finding my house" thing and he doesn't really see the need to go through this rigmarole.

Usually, if at a party or wanting to impress someone, Roops would employ an extravagant explanation using long words to describe what is to all intents and purposes a "relationship manager" but he's only had four hours sleep and needs to conserve what little brain power he has left.

Also, Roops doesn't really believe that this taxi driver has it in him to understand what a "relationship manager" is. He tried it once and immediately had to contend with two eyes staring at him through the rear view mirror saying "Yer a whit?!?", then giving Roops a suspicious once over as if resizing his masculinity followed by a suspicious, accusing glare which suggested he now thought his company was actually a front for an exotic dating agency.

Instead, and with considerable experience at this, Roops resorts to a one word answer which he thinks will quickly satisfy the taxi driver's curiosity, letting him get back to finding an ever more obscure way of getting them both to airport.

"Investment" Roops says.

Now it's not a complete lie to say that Roops works in investment. He does work in the procurement area of this large bank meaning that he has responsibility for investing their - and now by extension, the taxpayers' - money.

For that reason, he often says he's in the "area of investment" without actually doing investment in the classic "Buy/Sell" Gordon Gekko/Wall Street type of way. In other words, Roops is no more in investment than the box office attendant at the cinema is in the film industry.

29

The answer though is mere fodder to the taxi driver. Roops is now "game" because the taxi driver thinks he has a kindred spirit because lo and behold, is he not an expert in all matters economic, political and of course, investment? They're long lost financial troubadours flung together by chance on their fantastic voyage of discovery.

As far as Roops could translate, the questions went along the lines of "What's a double dip? What does he really think of bankers? What does he think of interest rates? Will the economy recover? Did Roops realise that the taxi driver could only afford three holidays this year? The price of fuel is shocking – will they give a tax break? This lot in power are a shower – do you get any inside knowledge of the Government? Labour were no better of course – who do you think is to blame for the economic crisis? What shares are you investing in? Do you have any tips? Is Japan doing well? Did Obama know what he was doing? Could Clinton have been trusted? There's too much cheap labour in this country but I can't believe we've voted for Brexit. Trump makes some good points but his hair is hilarious and as for his Twitter ..." and so it goes on.

Roops just decides to stare at his iPhone, his head spinning. "How on earth could he possibly answer any of that??"

Now it could just be sleep deprivation and the standard of chat flooding from the mouth of the driver, but every minute now feels like two and what should be a 15 minute journey now seems like an eternity and of course, they already had a delayed start.

Roops is in no mood for anyone getting in his way but he's already scuppered as he starts to think ahead to the queue building up at airport security which in turn will mean he has virtually no chance of getting his favourite single seat in the airport Lounge. He's getting more and more agitated and impatient.

He'd love to think that it can only get better from here but of course, the taxi journey hasn't quite finished with its bag of tricks yet. Oh no, they're only just approaching the airport and that triggers an unconscious streaming of bile and hatred towards the airport administrators from the taxi driver!

"Dae ye ken, this lot are absolute thieving bastards! Charge you for anything! £1 fur drap aff, £3.90 - THREE POUNDS FUCKING NINETY!! - tae pick ye up again! They're driving people to the fucking trams … welcome to Embra, ma erse …!"

In times of less stress, or if a day ever arrived that he actually cared, Roops would be tempted to point out to him that not only is Edinburgh Airport now the country's leading and most profitable airport, but the car parks appear to be completely full and they themselves are currently stuck in a lengthy queue trying to get into the Drop Off area - all of which represents an openly visible contradiction to the driver's theory.

But, well, to be truthful, he just can't be arsed. He's too tired and any attempt at thwarting the driver's argument will only result in further delays.

Roops instead nods and offers a conciliatory "humph" to acknowledge the taxi drivers wisdom. He just wants this over.

But sitting with his iPhone in hand brings on Roops's very worst trait, the angry email. If there is one thing that maturity hasn't dulled in him, it's the ability to compose the most inappropriate emails to anyone who crosses his path at any point of the day. He just rarely sends them now.

Roops starts composing a note to the Head of NeverFindU Taxis, Edinburgh:

"Dear Sir or Madam,

I feel compelled to write to you in light of recent engagements I've had with your taxi company. It is only because I have the future of your company at heart that I do this and I hope you find my constructive feedback helpful in your attempts at continuing to build a successful business.

You will see from my records that I am a regular user of your firm. This is not necessarily through choice – it's because you appear to have duped my organisation into thinking that you're a credible provider of transport services for members of its staff.

I'm not entirely sure of the procurement process you were asked to go through, but I'm willing to believe that it didn't actually involve you needing to demonstrate either the ability to pick someone up from their address at an agreed time nor indeed deliver them in a timely fashion to their destination. This is a flaw in our internal processes which I shall ask to be addressed separately.

You may think it's not for me to comment but I wonder if the overall experience of your customers might be improved if you could undertake some basic training with your drivers. For example, you may want to teach them to tell the time. This should improve their chances of picking up their passengers on time by a factor of at least 1000%.

You may also want to let your drivers know that the main dangers they face in carrying out their duties are usually right in front of them – therefore looking over their shoulder to talk to me whilst hurtling down the City Bypass at 85mph is not recommended. Your Health and Safety Officer may have a manual on this.

Additionally, I've noticed that most of your cabs have small black vents in the interior side panels. I've often tried to attract your driver's attention to the switch on their dashboard with the word "HEATER" on it. If they press this, just the once, you will find that the cases of hypothermia reported in your taxis decrease. The same could be said about the window switch marked "UP".

Finally, and you may think that I'm being particularly pedantic here but it would be quite pleasant if your drivers followed what some laughingly call "the quickest route".

I appreciate that you are a business and that its survival depends upon profit, however the route from Morningside in Edinburgh to the airport shouldn't normally take in western parts of Glasgow nor indeed cross the Forth Road Bridge – twice.

I am as always more than happy to sit down and discuss these points with you.

Yours faithfully,

Rupert X Wardhaugh"

Chapter 4
Teenage Wildlife

When getting closer to the airport terminal, Roops did at least have the comfort that everything from that point onwards should roughly work to a timetable because the entire transport infrastructure relied on it. Unlike the variety and vagaries of the taxi journey, there should be no room for manoeuvre now.

Airports have to work to an order otherwise there would be chaos.

That's the theory of course - the reality is entirely different and although Roops knew that's what should happen, it very rarely did.

For people who like order, such as Roops, they're always looking for reassurance that this very functional part of their day is working to time. Roops would immediately home in on the signs to check for both news of his flight and also the other flights heading to the same destination. Experience told him that most flight delays happened in clusters and were usually due to a weather related problem - so if an airport is affected for one flight, it's often impacted for all flights.

The volume of signs available for him to do this is perfect. It's Roops's equivalent of a big warm snuggly comfort blanket that says "We're not going to mess up your day today".

But of course, Roops's journey through the airport is far from smooth because he's not going to be surrounded by like-minded people. You see, there are broadly two types of traveller at an airport. There are people like Roops, who are largely anonymous as they enter the building just wanting to get from A to B as quickly and as quietly as possible. And then, there are the holidaymakers.

As Roops's taxi draws up to the Drop Off Zone at the airport, there is an almost audible sinking of his heart when, in early May, the first sign of summer is visible to him.

"Aw fuck" he says to himself, when his eyes scan down towards the entrance to the terminal building. "This is not going to be good."

The rising of grey whitish smoke has to some, a religious connotation – it's a reminder of the moment when the Papal conclave announces to the world "We have a Pope!" However, in early May at 5.15am there is no mistaking the significance of the billowing of smoke outside the airport terminal.

November to April is generally regarded as the season when largely middle-class families take second holidays to remote parts of mountainous Europe. They are usually well behaved, civilised and experienced travellers. Many of course are normally business travellers themselves taking a well-earned break who move their families through security and customs with military precision in deference, pity (and a little patronage) to their fellow breed.

Come May however, there is a seismic shift as the first discount flights to the nether regions of Europe begin. This early morning cloud of tobacco emissions, billowing into the eyes of innocent passers-by is the first sign of the seasonal change. Like the first swallow of summer, the pall of smoke from multiple draws of Regal King Size heralds a new dawn.

For a moment, Roops's heart lifts as he fools himself into false hope. Maybe this is actually some exhaust fumes from the Airport

Buses parked just outside the terminal building. They let off smoke after all?

But of course, this is indeed false hope indeed – tiredness will do that.

Deep down, Roops knew the truth. He knew that he should always have trusted his first instinct and as final confirmation of his worst fears, a quick scan at the mass of people delivers that final, unforgiving fact.

There are more football tops than suits ...

Imagine coming home and finding twenty squatters sitting in your front room, drinking your beer and holding your television remote control – that's what this feels like to Roops. He feels like his own home, his space and his clean air have all been wrestled from him.

For people like Roops, there is nothing more annoying, frustrating and disturbing than the budget flight holidaymaker. If you can imagine what it must be like to be a Sherpa who wakens up one day to find Everest full of another batch of hopeful mountaineers and worse again, their tons upon tons of junk, then that's what this is like.

When Roops sees this he knows that things are going to be pretty awful inside.

True to form, the airport is filled with people who make a conscious decision that it's entirely fine and socially acceptable to drink pints of lager at 5.30am and whose peacock-like plumage takes the form of a cacophony of tattoos. Conversation is a wasted commodity. Shouting and raucous laughter appears to be by far the preferred method of communication.

36

Roops thought back to his last encounter with the budget holidaymakers. It was a time when he vowed to avoid travelling from airports at this time of year again - but of course, he actually had no control over this and in any case, his memory had been wiped of that pain until now when it came flooding back.

The previous Spring, Roops was on a budget flight himself meaning he couldn't sit in his normal position in the Business Lounge. Instead he sat in horror, in a coffee shop which lined the main Departure Hall giving him a prime viewing platform to observe exactly what went on around him.

Roops sat transfixed, staring at these people with complete and utter disdain. It looked like an old episode of "It's A Knockout", essential viewing to him and his dad when he was growing up, but these were no fake oversized foam costumes in front of him. These were real, grown men lumbering towards the nearest bar in search of that first pint of lager. In his head, he imagined the voice of Eddie Waring laughing away whilst standing at the sides offering scores out of ten with a semi-glamorous girl holding the joker card.

These guys didn't even seem to need the benefit of eyesight marching like salivating beasts in procession towards the bar.

In another part of the Departure area, in comparison to a wildlife documentary, the central pride of the families were where the women dutifully tended to building their own camp made up of luggage strewn across as wide an area as possible in anticipation of the return of their males. Whilst waiting, they tended to their offspring's early morning meal.

With the voice of David Attenborough now playing in his head, Roops heard the commentary of the mealtime routine:

"And here we are, the mother lovingly preparing a meal of meat and fish in preparation of the mass migration to a new territory, knowing that this might be their last meal for at least twenty minutes. The young devour everything in their sight as they nuzzle into their mother's breast fighting to get the last crumbs of the barbecue beef and prawn cocktail crisps."

"She's obviously thinking that covers at least two of her five a day," thought Roops. "I'm sure there are some mango, raspberry and lime Bacardi Breezers on hand to complete the day's quota."

Within half an hour, further generations of the family gather together in attendance, from the 15 year old daughter (and her own children) all of the way up to the great-grandmother who had deserted her wheelchair in Lazarus-type fashion and was leading the conga through Duty Free singing "Hey Macarena!".

"Well at least we know what happened to the Bacardi Breezers" smiled Roops.

All this before they'd even been near a plane. Roops despaired as he remembered there was a very strong chance he might end up on the same plane as them.

So it was with this memory fresh in his mind that Roops entered the terminal building with justifiable trepidation. He felt physically sick knowing the hell that probably awaited him. But before that he still had to make his way through the security area! He really hated travelling at this time of year.

"None of them can even understand basic civil questions, let alone read" he thought to himself, close to tears. "Security's going to be a nightmare today."

Now Roops is an enormous jazz fan. He loves the spikiness of the music, the fact that they are a series of notes which individually shouldn't sit alongside each other yet somehow just work when played in the right environment, with the right instruments and of course, exceptionally talented musicians. It's not melodic in the traditional sense – it can be sharp, or even just sound plain wrong. It can sound disjointed, directionless but at the same time, progressive, relaxing and rhythmic.

"Working your way through airport security is like that too" he would say, "just without the talent. And it lacks the rhythm. Nothing in the security area works to any order, nobody really seems to know what is going on and yet, miraculously you somehow pop out at the other end! I've no idea how they do it but worse than that, I don't think they know how they do it either."

"It's genuinely just like listening to jazz. It can be a tortuous experience, it can last from anywhere between 10 minutes to an hour and a half, and you're often left sweating and gasping for air. At times I need cold water and a blast of oxygen just to stabilise myself at the end of it all! Have you ever listened to Bitches Brew? When you do, you'll think you're in the middle of the airport security ..." he would opine.

Still, there was a certain logic to his theory (however far fetched).

Roops arrived at the entrance to the airport security area with one thought in his mind ... "This is just going to be one almighty fuck up".

He'd spent so many hours in this area, he felt he could predict this with the same level of confidence as when he said "Dad, I don't like that Stuart Hall bloke".

It was a racing certainty. A stick on.

Combining the jazz routines laid down by the security people with the semi-comatose state of the budget airline entourage was of course the basis for Roops' prediction. This was a road he'd been down so often before that he knew that if Betfair was to offer odds, they'd be slimmer than the piece of tissue he was currently using to dab the tears away from his eyes in trepidation of what lay ahead.

Thankfully for Roops, getting through security is eased, a bit, by the introduction of the "Fast Track" queue. He never ever feels guilty about using this queue. True, it was like airport apartheid, the "them and us" but to those who can use it, it's bliss. Roops would often scan across the vast security hall and shudder in horror feeling like he was watching car crash TV.

"I'm so glad I'm not over there right now," he would think, "I've been in their shoes and it's hell."

In return, he would be faced with a multitude of scowling foreheads, piercing eyes through a curtain of more piercings, staring back and jealously mouthing "You smug, elitist bastard. You'll be standing right next to us in roughly 30 seconds". Which of course, is precisely what happens.

Whilst the Fast Track gives some benefits, it's no guarantee to a completely easy life and of course, the security people like to ply misery on everyone who passes through their door. They don't discriminate at all.

"What sort of job advert is written for a person doing a job like this?" Roops thought whilst standing watching the complete and absolute disintegration of all human courtesy around him.

"It must be something like:
Do you:

- Hold a grudge for roughly three years
- Get really annoyed that someone else appears to be happier than you
- Enjoy rubbing your hands under sweaty armpits
- Enjoy causing the ultimate humiliation of raking through other people's clothing and dirty underwear in full view of a hundred other people
- Have absolutely no concept of how to run an efficient process?"

Who applies for a job like that? Who reads that advert and says "That's me!! I'm just the fella for that!"

There appeared to be roughly thirty of them all around him.

Now what Roops liked most about being in the Fast Track queue was that most of the people in front of him were also likely to be regular travellers. That means, they've been through security so many times that it's like second nature and naturally, they know the drill in advance.

"Have your jacket off, remove your belt, take your laptop out of its case, ensure all liquids are in the see-through bag and of course, make sure that none of it is more than 100ml" has been shouted at them in militaristic fashion hundreds of times.

Of course, even then, the security staff can't resist having their little bit of fun.

Oh no, not when they look and see the slightly expanded waist of the middle aged men straining against the edge of their by now belt-less trousers. Roops would watch and squirm as he saw the whole scene playing out in front of his eyes.

It would start with what appeared to be a simple enough request. "Can you remove your shoes please?"

Of course, if you were Nadia Comaneci this would be no problem at all. But nobody in the airport right at that moment is. This simple enough question suddenly becomes a trial of human endeavour.

Removing your shoes in the comfort of your own home or hotel room is relatively easy given the availability of seating and an element of privacy to allow as many involuntary noises as it normally takes to remove a pair of sturdy brogues. But this is an airport security area and it seems that seating is prohibited. Even the flimsy plastic grey ones.

So at the point the poor soul in front of you is asked to remove their shoes, they're already holding their hand luggage and their toiletries in each hand, and their belt is rolled up and held between the second and third fingers. They now have to untie their shoelaces, then bend over to pull off their shoes, pick each up and then place them in the smaller of the two trays.

With no seats around and a suit which is slightly straining at the waist, this poor soul has to effectively touch his toes which is something he's probably been neither asked to do nor able to do since he'd been at Primary School doing PE in his underpants.

This impending humiliation has resulted in such a strong sweat that by now, his shoes are welded to his feet as he's trying to work out just how the hell he was going to do all of this without ripping the arse out of his trousers.

There is no glamour in this process. It's not simple and it's not graceful as the chap needs to not only negotiate getting down to his feet but getting back to an upright position again. A loud fart remains a distinct possibility to signal the final movement of the process.

"It's no wonder you never saw Nadia Comaneci in a pair of brogues ...!!" thought Roops.

Looking over to the other part of security always confused Roops. The need for additional security shouldn't be a great surprise to anyone with a television set (unless of course it's permanently set to The Racing Channel) he thought. If by some chance, as a passenger, you weren't aware of the atrocities which the security forces are keen to avoid ever happening again, the ever thoughtful people at the airport very kindly advise you of the correct "security protocol" at least 54 times between the front door of the airport and the security area itself.

But when he looked over at the long and winding queue, he couldn't help but wonder what all the people were doing while standing there. What were they looking at and were they taking everything in?

What he could never comprehend was the incredible look of shock on the faces of some as they are asked to remove their extensive collection of jewellery, rings, bracelets, necklaces as well as their belts, coats, boots etc.

Roops was exasperated by all of this, on one occasion even engaging in conversation with one of "them".

"Excuse me madam, I'm interested. As you stood in this queue for the last thirty minutes, looking around you and watching what everyone else was doing, what did you think you were going to be asked to do when you reached the front?"

"Oh I don't travel very often, son" came the reply.

"Right, but did you think it was just random requests to remove all metallic items? Didn't you see every single person in front of you doing the same thing?"

"I'm sorry, I don't really understand …?"

"Why did you look so surprised when you were asked to remove your jewellery and why were you so underprepared?"

"Oh, is that what they were doing?" she said.

"Madam, you've more metal on you than Steptoe had in his backyard and you're claiming you don't remember ever being asked to remove it before when you travelled and you couldn't see everyone else in front of you being asked to remove it either?" exclaimed Roops.

"Oh don't worry about it" quickly realising that not only was this a futile exercise, but he was only delaying his own progress. "Enjoy your flight …"

Nowadays, Roops just watches and observes. Engagement clearly doesn't work. It was almost as if he was speaking a completely different language.

He stood in the security queue and couldn't help but be struck by the irony that was all around him. Everywhere he looked had adverts of people enjoying their experience of being in the airport. Holograms smiling pleasantly as he was asked to prepare for the impending search of his possessions.

This irony of course, was two-fold. Not only is the experience anything but pleasant, but from the look of some of the people around him and perhaps about to be sitting next to at 30,000 feet in the air, Roops never felt in the slightest bit "secure".

But he did thank himself for small mercies. Because that wasn't his worst nightmare he faced when he got to security. That experience was usually, on a relative basis, short and sharp.

They were just the warm up. There was one sight which Roops dreaded even more, a sight which generally welcomes you in mid-October, mid-April and sometimes early-July …

Hundreds of little fuckers swarming in every direction like a disturbed nest of wasps, finally free from the loving bosom of their parents and the daily discipline of their school environment. Free to maraud new territory, to touch everything that comes into their immediate reach, to ignore every instruction given to them, to avoid all protocol, queuing system and even people around them.

The school trip is by some distance, the very worst sight that Roops could cast his weary eyes upon when reaching the security hall of an airport.

He hated every single one of them. All of them recognisable by the matching hoodies, identified individually by the names emblazoned on their backs – Kourtney, Jaydn, Shaznay. Names that looked more at home on the Countdown conundrum board than on a birth certificate.

Backpacks hanging around their knees, noise just exuding from their every pour, none of them having yet mastered the art of walking in a straight line without their mouths gaping wide open and snot streaming from their noses.

Standing behind them in a security queue is the worst possible thing that can be inflicted on a business traveller. And the sadistic bastards working in security know this – you can see them stifle their laughter, watching your barely disguised hatred towards

"Shanice" (according to its hoodie top) as she struggles to understand the basic rudiments of placing items in a grey tray.

"Anything metallic needs to go into the tray."
"What's metallic? Are my rings metallic?"

"Do you have any liquids with more than 100ml"
"Eh? What's 100ml? My mum gave me this bottle of Irn Bru – is that even liquid …?"

And so on and so on … hundreds of them, swarming around causing absolute chaos and confusion with no social order in sight.

Roops would stare at them, wondering whether all of them actually make it through the whole trip ahead of them or whether it's just accepted as collateral damage that a few will be mislaid along the way. Nobody seems to be holding any authority over them or seems to care what they're up to. They're just left to roam and shout at each other.

Roops couldn't wait to get through security and to have his usual fun with the little, push button thing which asks about his experience. It's very simple and consists of one question and three optional answers.

The question is something like "How was your experience of the security area today?"

Now knowing their audience, they've clearly decided that the question in itself used up more words than the average Neanderthal can process in a day, especially when their number one agenda is to race to the bar. So helpfully, they help the process of answering by using pictures, namely a happy face on a green button, an unemotional face on an orange button and a sad face on a red button.

In other words, no need for speaking or writing. Just press a button that most closely matches your mood at that point in time. Or just press your favourite colour if that's what you prefer to do.

Even getting most of them to understand this was highly optimistic Roops would think. He wouldn't be surprised if most of them press the orange button only because it's the one that most closely resembles their teenage daughter and her newly sprayed fake tan.

Of course, complaining about the painful process he'd just been through - face to face, with a real human being - would be completely pointless. Roops knew that it didn't matter how angry and frustrated he might be, the awfulness of what he'd just gone through was probably best forgotten as quickly as he could. He just needed to move on.

Complaining face to face only backfires because all you're doing is delaying yourself even more. You're the one who needs to catch a plane and they know that.

So apart from the sheer relief of getting to press the little red face to register just how awful a time you'd had (and if you listen very carefully, you can hear cheering from the sadists controlling this whole area when you do), there's no recourse. You can't undo a poor experience.

Undeterred, and stoked up by an anger bordering on combustion, Roops looked around him and started thinking about an email he'd love to send to the Head of Airport Security. This would be his masterpiece, he thought. This would nail the bastard to the mast and humiliate him in the same way that he seems to instruct his staff to do on a daily basis ...

"This email will need my complete focus" thought Roops as he sat down, cracked his knuckles and got down to business.

"Dear Sir or Madam,

I do hope that this letter finds you well. By that, I mean finds you at all, since legend of your existence ranks alongside the Loch Ness Monster and Bigfoot. We've heard that people manage the security area but all evidence and intuition suggests otherwise.

I don't mean to begin by sounding rude however having stood in the queues to get through security at your airport for close to 30 minutes, rudeness is coming naturally to me because I've had it thrown at me in every direction. So naturally, as a result of my environment I find that I'm becoming more and more irritable.

I did think about pressing the "red frowning face" on your feedback machine but I wasn't convinced that this would truly reflect the utter contempt I have for the alleged process that you seem to be operating in the security hall. Pressing the "red frowning face" button three times in quick succession really hard doesn't either. In fact, I'd probably need to hit the "red frowning face" with a sledge hammer and then furiously stamp on the shattering pieces falling to the ground to properly reflect the anger and frustration I feel right now ...

That said, I was always taught to be constructive with my feedback and now that I've had time to reflect, I've thought about some suggestions to possibly offer passengers a more positive experience when travelling through your unit.

1) *It's important that staff are happy at work. Studies have shown that happiness releases endorphins which can improve the mental state of individuals allowing them to have a more positive and healthy outlook on life. Therefore, you might want to think about resetting some of your staff objectives. "Pissing off as many people as possible", "Opening up embarrassing items of luggage" and "Avoiding all evidence of basic human courtesy" might not be regarded as "positive".*

On the other hand, "Being polite" and "Smiling more" are generally targets which might improve the working environment for your staff which in turn might improve everyone's experiences. I mean Jesus, the odd smile wouldn't hurt anyone! (Laughing when you pull a dildo out of someone's hand luggage doesn't count, by the way!)

2) *Queues – I appreciate that this can be tricky but as a measure, a queue of people stretching back out of the hall door for roughly 100 metres might be classified as a "long queue." This in turn means that you are likely to have a higher proportion of "angry travellers" increasing the chance of someone being rude to your staff who, we are consistently told, "are only trying to do their job".*

I noticed that although you seem to have 6 large x-ray machines, only 2 ever seem to be used. Might "switching the others on" play a part in speeding up the number of passengers who pass through the hall? That might even encourage some of them to press the "green happy smiling face" button on your feedback machine. Maybe even some of the people wearing uniforms but who tend to stand around the sides of the hall could help out?

3) *Forward planning – similar to the point above. I can't help notice from my regular travel that there are a lot of flights in the morning. I'm no expert but I'm assuming that this in turn means more passengers, meaning potentially more queues ... do you see where I'm going with this one? Maybe get more people working in the morning ...??*

4) *Have you ever thought about aligning your queues based on IQ? Please ...?*

As ever, I'm more than happy to discuss any points within this. Assuming you actually care.

Yours faithfully,

Rupert X Wardhaugh"

Chapter 5
Slip Away

In spite of his years of travelling, Roops still had some semblance of domesticity, living with his family and his little dog, a French bulldog, which far from being the most fearful creature, at least could be picked up and warm his lap on a cold winter's night. It also doesn't drool in the way that a Labrador would, meaning less embarrassing marks on his shoes and lower trouser legs.

Roops absolutely loved sitting in his garden, doing nothing in particular, staring at the sky and just generally having some "me time". The last thing on his mind was work or travelling.

On one afternoon, Roops was sitting in his back garden, with his dog, watching a colony of ants marching back and forward collecting crumbs of food – food which he thought looked like small crumbs but to these ants must have seemed like boulders.

He was convinced he'd seen something similar in one of those documentaries that he liked to watch and here it was, being played out in his very own back garden.

It was a familiar scene. The ants marching back and forth, like an army meticulously following the same route, all at the same pace, occasionally bumping into each other but then politely giving way so as not to impede the progress of their fellow worker. In Roops's mind, he could almost imagine their politeness to each other being similar to an old 1940s' film with a doffing of their cap and some 'scuse me Guv'nor repartee.

Sometimes for really big bits of food, they would work in teams. This harmonious collaboration which comes completely naturally to them with apparently no arguments or nonsense about who goes to the front and who's at the back and so on. Roops sat for ages amazed to watch nature in action like this, finding the whole thing absolutely fascinating.

He was intrigued and went onto his phone to read up some more on their behaviour. He wanted to read about the hierarchy (since he didn't really trust the Disney version of the story that he'd been compelled to sit through with his nieces once) and in particular, he wanted to know how they know which way to go when the scouts find food.

He was astonished to read that they secrete a trail when they walk which allows them and others to follow the prescribed route. This is how they know which way to go and which way to return following an almost exact route. It's astonishingly clever - if a little gross at the same time.

"Maybe that's how some of these families I see at the airport manage to find their way around!" he thought. "Could they actually be walking around with leaking Tena underwear??"

So on that afternoon, under the summer sun Roops became really attached to his little trail of ants. He even tried to make up a little story of who each one was, what their relationship to each other was, what they were planning to do that evening and so forth.

Boredom soon set in though particularly as it became quite difficult to identify each one being as they all basically looked exactly the same as each other.

So Roops poured some poison over them.

The ants all went absolutely mad. Not angry (although he never doubted for a second that they weren't completely enamoured with the situation) but mad in the way that they all started scurrying around in every direction. No longer moving back and forward along one line, they were running at different speeds, in different directions and at different angles. It was almost like the reverse of what happens when you place a magnet under iron filings. These guys just scattered.

Two things went through Roops's head as to why this happened:

1. The poison had wiped out the scent of the trail that they had secreted so they no longer had their "vision" to follow. Their natural radar and compass had been affected or:
2. They were really pissed off that someone had poured poison over them and they were freaking out.

Of course, Roops wasn't able to ask them himself but slowly one by one they stopped scuttling around and he had to brush them away, his fun over for one afternoon. But their behaviour stayed in his memory for some time. He'd seen something like this elsewhere.

****

Having now successfully negotiated the security process, Roops' mind turned to getting to the Departure Lounge and quickly. Not just the normal Lounge of course – his aim was to get to the Executive Lounge, his haven, his oasis. Coffee, toast, yoghurt, pastries, fruit and a choice of newspapers - The Times, The Telegraph, The FT or even, if no one is watching, the Daily Mail.

Most importantly, there are very, very few holidaymakers in there. The few that are, invariably being business travellers themselves, at least know how to behave.

But even this leg of the trip wasn't an easy journey to undertake.

Roops had a theory though about airport management. That was that in spite of being one of their most regular customers, airport management don't actually like business travellers very much because invariably when they're there, they don't spend very much money.

Business travellers might stretch to a coffee and a bun very occasionally but that's about it. They're not there to laze around, wander from shop to shop and buy tickets for supercar raffles. They most likely want to hide inside the Executive Lounge away from the bustle before getting on their plane.

Holidaymakers on the other hand, high on the anticipation of their trip are positively flowing with money and aren't scared to use it. If there was a weather report for the airport it would say "It's raining tenners in the Duty Free Shop". Holidaymakers will buy any old tat and modern airports aren't slow to offer said tat to anyone who'll take notice.

A recently new phenomenon to hit UK airports is putting the Duty Free shop right at the exit of the security hall. The Duty Free shop opens its arms in fake adoration to tempt the holidaymaker, still battered and weakened from their experience of the security process, with promises of cheap fags and cheaper still vodka.

If they played a voiceover of the Wicked Witch beckoning Dorothy with her "Come here my beauty" call you wouldn't be in the slightest bit surprised. The Duty Free shop lures and seduces all before them from the crusty old hags needing thousands of cigarettes to support them through the next fortnight, to the innocent teenagers, mercilessly entranced by the smells of the latest celebrity endorsed perfumes. Fagin himself couldn't have laid a better trap.

The problem here is that these distractions have an incredible impact on the typical holidaymaker who seem to fall into a strange trance like state, walking around in every possible direction with absolutely no logic applied.

Up to that point of course, they've been channelled along queuing systems because they basically can't be trusted to get from A to B without veering off in every direction (although obviously the queuing system is also designed by sadistic security staff who just love watching people get really pissed off before they get to go on their holidays.)

Being released from this queuing system means the typical holidaymakers just scatter in every direction and it's genuinely immediate – it's a cross between"Night of the Living Dead" and Michael Jackson's "Thriller". There doesn't appear to be any order to the direction that they walk or consciousness of anything or anyone around them.

To be fair, only those with any degree of mobility get do this but this doesn't deter the the elderly from laying down a different trap altogether.

In what looks like something straight out of a Sandhurst training manual, the elderly and infirm, as one, walk really, really, really slowly, generally four abreast, to cover the full width of the walkway. They walk so slowly that you genuinely wonder whether they've lapsed into an energy saving mode. Trolley cases are used as additional barriers for anyone looking to audaciously circumnavigate them.

Meanwhile, the younger ones (and this term "younger" is used in a completely liberal and relative sense) walk around aimlessly bouncing from aisle to aisle like balls in a pinball machine.

It's as if they've never seen so many different types of perfume, sunglasses and alcohol together under the one roof. It drives them crazy, possessed even, and throws what last reserves of directional ability they had useless. They wander from side to side, mouths gaping at the Aladdin's Cave of discounts, seduced by bold signs promising "20% off High Street Prices" for a box of M&M's shaped like a large yellow blob or for a tin of shortbread inside a toy London bus. The things you really need in life.

In addition to this, the people who design these shops lay a special pathway into the floor in an attempt to gently guide you through the various parts of the shop trying to indicate what is the main thoroughfare and where you venture into shopping space. It's like a big lazy river or even the Yellow Brick Road leading you to Oz – except it's mostly black in colour with little twinkly bits through it.

This pathway lures you into believing it's your friend but it has one cynical little trick up its sleeve.

Conscious that not all people beating its path will be drawn towards the special edition 67% proof vodka, the black surface of this walkway is polished to such a high degree that you'd need the combined skill and balance of Torvill & Dean, Robin Cousins and perhaps even John Curry to get along it at any reasonable pace.

It's like walking on sheer ice and as soon as you need to quicken your pace or change your direction, it snaps at you, risking serious or permanent injury.

Roops hates this bit. For him with his polished shoes and leather soles it's treacherous, whereas the holidaymakers, in their sports gear and rubber soled trainers, skip along with as firm a grip as an F1 car in brand new tyres.

So whilst Roops is left there trying to find a route around the elderly parked across the floor and trying to time the gaps in between the flying meteorites of the younger passengers bouncing around the room, he also needs to balance himself perfectly just to avoid looking like Bambi taking his first steps.

When coming around the corner of this precinct he spots the tills ahead of him, representing an enormous relief not only for his sanity but for his hips. The tills double up as his finishing line where he finally, hopefully, gets to break free from this slippery, sliding hell.

"At last" he gasps "not far to go before I get some space, oxygen and for fuck's sake, some grip under my feet."

At this point, he isn't even thinking about how he's going to make it through from there to the Executive Lounge. Roops almost wants to dive over the final part of the shopping area as if he was straining to win an Olympic gold medal, bruised by the constant dancing and weaving just to stay upright and to avoid bumping into the legions of jogging bottomed shoppers.

Chapter 6
Velvet Goldmine

When Roops finally arrives at the front door of the Executive Lounge, it's like a second home for him representing familiarity and even civilisation.

He looks breathless and slightly traumatised, as he hands over his mobile phone to get his boarding pass scanned.

"Hello again" says the familiar voice behind the counter.

"Hi there, how are you? It's murder out there." he gasped.

He couldn't believe he was actually just referring to an airport Duty Free shop - it was more like he was taking on the role of a Sky News reporter, or even Kate Adie, from some far off war zone.

Mrs Lounge Lady just laughed at him "You're not the first today who's said that. We're quite quiet in here so far …"

"Probably because they're all still out there!" laughed Roops. "It's not good. I think I saw men go down … we should think about informing their families."

Reaching the Lounge was significant for Roops. For a start, it was his first chance to sit down since getting out of the taxi. More importantly, it was an opportunity to finally have some peace and quiet. This was undoubtedly his Base Camp no matter what he thought before.

Even although the thought of slightly stale muesli with strands of someone else's hair isn't too appealing, at this point it's as welcoming to Roops as the milk from a mother's breast must be to a new born baby. In fact, the milk on offer is like the milk from a mother's breast but that's because it's probably been lying out for a week.

The Executive Lounge, although a relative idyll, is quite a strange place. It's as familiar to Roops as his own front room but also quite tribal at the same time. Everyone in there has been through the same experience as Roops to reach it and there's a sort of "we've been through hell but survived it" mentality amongst the people as they stumble through the door, engaging in gentle and familiar chit-chat with the cheery, uniformed staff at the door.

But even in here, Roops was wound up. When you're in this sort of environment, there are rules. They're not written down anywhere but there is a certain standard of behaviour that is expected from everyone using the place.

And this is what really got to Roops especially after everything that he'd been through. Some people just didn't know the rules or indeed, chose not to follow the rules.

"They're needed otherwise there would be chaos. Anarchy even!" he thought.

The Lounge wasn't just for sitting in and chatting to fellow passengers after all. It had to be respected as did those who used it.
Roops hadn't spent years of mental torture travelling around the UK at stupid times of the day and in all kinds of weather to share the Lounge with people who didn't respect "the Rules".

He was very clear on this. They weren't written down but perhaps they needed to be.

In one of his more extreme moments, after a particularly arduous journey from the front of the airport, Roops sat down muttering "Right, that's it - I'm going to have to write some bloody rules for this place and send them to the folk that run it ... too many people are coming in here and spoiling things. Enough is enough. We need to do something about this."

Roops sat down and listed "the Rules" - at least, his Rules - in preparation for another email being fired out:

a) *Find a seat first, preferably not right next to someone else (because nobody wants you near them);*

b) *Don't hog the coffee machine – they are interminably slow as it is so just order a simple coffee please; Will extra froth on your latte really make that much difference at 0600?*

c) *Never take the newspaper that sits on top of the pile – always try to grab one at least three down to cause absolute chaos for everyone else;*

d) *If you're slightly overweight, it's not cool to leave the shirt button closest to your belly button undone. The Lounge does not offer Gorilla Salad for breakfast for a reason. Put the hairy button away please;*

e) *Don't eat the fruit – it's only there for decoration and to add some colour to the place. There's no need to be a show off and imply that you're actually healthy. We know it's just a front and you gorge on stodge as much as the rest of us;*

f) *Toast is always in short supply – so when more is laid out, remember to be totally selfish and show complete disregard for your fellow travellers. Take as much as you can in one visit;*

g) *If it's announced that your flight is delayed, remember to sigh really deeply and loudly in a way to imply that you are more impacted than everyone else around you.*

In other words, let the world know just how incredibly important (you think) you are and bray like a donkey;

h) *If people do happen to speak to you, they're only being polite. They're only likely to ask one question - "How are you?" - and similarly, they'll only actually expect one of two answers:*

    a. *"Oh, really busy" or;*

    b. *"Not bad for this time of day ..."*

i) *Never, ever, ever engage in meaningful conversation with people you bump into. They were only being polite when they said hello (refer to "h"). Don't make them regret ever making eye contact with you;*

"These Rules are there for a reason and designed to preserve the happiness and pettiness of all Lounge users."

Roops looked around at his fellow world weary travellers recognising what few outside of here actually realise - it's most certainly not the preserve of the elite. There are undoubtedly some in here who believe that because their company pays them to get on a flight at a ridiculous time of day, this somehow bestows upon them the title of "considerably better than everyone outside".

Most however are just like Roops, and don't particularly want to be up at 4am and just see this environment as a little bit of a reward for the pain they've just been through. It's almost as if the airline company has had a rare moment of humanity and decided to open this space like a dog owner would leave the car window open for their animal on a hot day.

Roops couldn't help observing what a miserable environment it actually was. It genuinely was just like a glorified holding pen, for people like him who just hate the world they live in, with admittedly comfortable seats and if the time of day is right, a plethora of free drink. But mostly in the morning their height of luxury is some lukewarm yoghurt and rancid coffee (which doubles as a fantastic laxative it has to be said).

It's not as if they're offering trendy rechauffe to the customers (unless you count the pain au raisins) or the sort of experience you'd expect if having breakfast at say, The Ritz. It was never meant to of course. It's merely the ego of certain people within there that think it should.

Roops sought out his favoured seat, in the corner, not on a natural route to the newspapers, coffee machine or toilets. In other words, where nobody would accidentally bump into him or even have to walk past him. These seats are in short supply though and any delay through security and the shopping area puts at risk his chances of securing one. There are very few seats in the Lounge which favour minimal human contact.

With one secured though, he looked around and could see most people still shaking off the effects of sleep deprivation and beginning to adopt the standard Lounge look of "being serious". They were after all business people and they're in an Executive Lounge so by definition, in their minds anyway, they needed to put on a facial display which shows everyone else just how very important they are. Very, very important. And very serious.

Watching them was more fascinating than any book on mind management or exercise in killing ants in his back garden for Roops. The Lounge users' time is spent staring at a phone or tablet, occasionally emitting a loud noise to display displeasure at some poor sod who has, as a result of significant fear, used up their weekend to compose an email delivering bad news. Or possibly, Roops had decided, they're reading a sports page but have developed this front to throw other travellers off the scent that they haven't actually received any meaningful correspondence for around three weeks.

Occasionally, Roops's eyes dart up towards the Departures Board just to check everything is fine. Gates used tend to be standard – number 5 for London City, number 11 for Gatwick and number 12 for Heathrow. If the airport dares interfere with this standard procedure then all hell lets loose … audible gasps abound and the Board stared at for an interminable time to study with disbelief if the London City flight is actually leaving from Gate 6! (This is the gate formerly used by the short lived Virgin Airways flight – so by definition, is regarded as the "really shit gate").

And then there is the ultimate nightmare. It's like seeing the Four Horsemen of the Apocalypse riding out from the horizon of the misty morning, when you look up and see the dreaded scrolling announcement saying "Flight Delayed".

For experienced travellers like Roops though, it's rare that this ever happens within a single announcement. Airports and airlines like to create a sense of drama which the regular traveller is now invariably wise to.

Roops looked up and could see that all the other flights going to London were now being called for boarding. This meant that there weren't any weather problems in the London area which in turn made it all the more suspicious that his flight was yet to be called. Even with 15 minutes until his scheduled take-off time, the flight details remained curiously quiet with the ominous message on the Board still just saying "Gate 5". Roops could smell a rat.

He flicked onto the airline website on his mobile which sometimes offers more information. Sure enough, estimated arrival for his flight appears to be in five hours time.

Now arithmetic was never his strongest point but even Roops could work out that if he was due to be landing in five hours time, for a flight that should barely last one hour then something's likely to be up.

Roops looked around the Lounge and began to see similarly suspicious and confused looks. Occasionally one person wanders to the front counter to ask for information.

This is obviously a futile exercise because the one thing airlines will never do is give you "more information". This is anathema to their existence. They are in the transportation business – a million miles from a customer service business. Your needs are not important to them so why on earth would they imply otherwise by offering "more information"?

Then Roops saw the Board switching from advising the gate number to a message saying "More information soon". This is a direct "piss take" because of course, as we know, the airlines don't like giving "more information".

"They're just goading us now" thought Roops. "They have so much power over us - I feel so weak." Roops hated them for it.

Then out of nowhere, and after what feels like forever, an estimated time of departure pops up varying between a one hour and three hour delay.

Roops knows that any "delay" shorter than one hour isn't really regarded as a delay – it's just a minor inconvenience in the mind of the airline. It's like being short-changed by 5p - not really worth bothering about is it?

In these circumstances, he'd normally just be directed to the plane which then just sits by the runway as if still asleep until it's finally allowed to go. The weary traveller has the pleasure of sitting on a plane which has no power meaning in the summer you are cooked alive through a lack of air conditioning and in the winter, frozen because the heating can't be switched on. The pilot explains that air traffic control have made him do this, the ultimate in "it's not my fault" excuses.

If the delay is longer than three hours for domestic flights, this inevitably means a full cancellation with the risk of aircraft being out of position all over Europe.

"The airlines should just front up and tell us that their timetable is more important than us!" Roops would fume. "I'm convinced that if airlines could operate without us, they probably would."

Whether it's a delay or cancellation, as one of the main rules of the Lounge states, it's at this point that you must start braying like a donkey and posturing in a manner which would make some think you'd mislaid your favourite child. Roops stood there, looking around him and watching all these grown adults making the most embarrassing noises and pulling the most stupid faces to do nothing other than display how incredibly important they think they are.

Now of course, it's true that his day has gone from being a bit screwed to screwed up completely, but at least Roops was able to maintain a certain level of dignity, or so he thought.

This delay at least allowed Roops to slump back in his chair and start to write an email. He can feel himself getting wound up by the circumstances he finds himself in, which is usually a sign of danger so he now knows to keep away from his work email. Going onto that would only result in him firing off an inappropriate missive which would merely underline what a lot of people already thought of him, he reckoned, which was that he was a patronising git with an overinflated ego.

He chooses to write his own personal email instead as a form of catharsis. This would help relieve his tension but it was important that he took his own advice and so he started to direct some of his ire at the people he thinks might be able to improve things for him in this situation. He writes an email to the people that run the Executive Lounge.

"Dear Sir or Madam,

I am a regular user of your Lounge which means that unfortunately, I need to fly a lot on business. It also means that I think I'm very, very important. And I adopt a very serious frown just in case you were ever in any doubt of this fact.

Your Lounge acts as a haven for me, keeping me safe and cosseted from the general hubbub of the public areas of the airport.

I like the fact that I can get a coffee fairly easily and you offer some things closely related to food which in turn, represents my first breakfast of the day.

But here's the thing. By the time I get to your Lounge, I'll have just fought my way past thousands of tracksuit wearing, size 18 people all drooling over cheap perfume and bright signs.

Immediately after leaving your Lounge, I'm going to be sat on a small aircraft with a hundred other people before getting on a train with hundreds of other people.

So it would be nice if I could have a small break from people. Just for a wee while.

Currently, I've found that the only way to do this is to lock myself in your toilet cubicle just to get a little bit of "me time". But I can't see the Departures screen from in there and also, I'm not sure that it does my chronic haemorrhoid problem any good.

Is there any chance you could set up a special area for people like me who appear to be socially inept first thing in the morning?

It'd probably be better for everyone and would free up one of your toilets for those with genuine bowel issues.

Best wishes

Rupert X Wardhaugh

p.s. When we ask your staff for "information" on a potentially delayed flight, we're not doing it as part of some Crystal Maze type quiz. It's not just for our own entertainment or because we just want someone to talk to. It's because we have a genuine need to know whether the rest of our day is going to be completely and utterly fucked up. So maybe you could get your guys to open up a bit? Ta.

p.p.s. I've enclosed some suggested Rules for users of the Lounge. If you wouldn't mind printing them off, maybe laminating them and posting them in the entrance way, I'm sure it will help everyone."

He sat back and read over his note with a huge grin on his face. It genuinely felt good to get that off his chest.

Chapter 7
Something In The Air

Finally, after what seems like hours of desperation and an intense information void, an announcement comes over the tannoy of the Lounge - "Ladies and gentlemen, flight BA8701 is now ready to board at gate 5 …". A collective relief descends.

Almost as one, the people in the Lounge rise and start their steady march towards the gate leaving their cosy haven to join the rest of the travellers. In all, there will be roughly 120 grown adults standing in a queue to board a plane.

This is a part of the routine that never failed to amuse Roops. These are mostly educated people - certainly educated to a standard that they could read (evidenced by the fact they've spent the last few hours staring at a phone/tablet/newspaper or swearing at the Departure Board) however their recent inertia has introduced a strange sense of paranoia.

You see, there seems to be an incredible rush to get to the front of the queue as if only those near the front stand any chance of actually getting on the plane.

When you consider that everyone in the airport has their own destination to get to it's unlikely that anyone without a boarding pass for the flight will be wanting to get on it. And similarly, everyone wanting to board this flight is already in possession of their own unique boarding pass - which displays its own unique seat number. So why the rush? Roops would step back and watch all of this scene reminiscent of news reports showing thousands of people with their faces pressed up against the doors of Harrods at the start of their traditional New Year's Day Sale (on December

24th), the smug security guards holding them back long enough to ensure they're also part of the early evening news.

Elbows grow larger, side glances more pronounced and of course the less than gentle exhalation of breath gives out one very clear message – "Get out of my way. This is my plane, my seat, my space and I'm getting on it NOW." Logic plays no part in this process nor do manners. There is a focus and concentration on the main goal like a boxer eyeing up his opponent at the start of the bout.

"Playing at adults today?" Roops would mutter under his breath, shaking his head in exasperation. "Overgrown, irrational, petulant kids."

To stir things up a bit, Roops would somehow find reason to stop and bend over to tie a shoelace, placing his bag just far enough away from him to lure a potentially embarrassing fall for anyone acting in an over zealous manner. He'd never make eye contact, purely because that would give his game away instead just smiling to himself.

"It's the little things in life!" he'd laugh to himself. "I just hope I've made you that little bit more pissed off". But, what really made him laugh was when they made all this effort to get to the front of a queue which didn't actually have a plane at the end of it - it was only a bus!

Airports don't like to makes things that easy for you so have introduced some novel disruptors of their own such as the stairwell, or indeed a bus.

Both are relatively self-explanatory but each makes a mockery of the experience that the airport and airline have tried to foist on you up to that point. They will have painted a picture of you floating through the security area, sauntering through the shops at your leisure whilst laughing with your kids as you marvel at the amazingly cheap deals on offer. It's an idyll which you rarely get to see whether you're a business traveller or even a holidaymaker.

In some airports, you get through the gate and literally have to stand in a stairwell with walls made of corrugated metal and no heating. There is no view save for the rear hairline of the person in front of you. You perch yourself on your own little step or even heaven forbid, one that you need to share with someone else.

You're unable to turn around because there is a lack of space and there's little indication of when you might actually get to board. Air quality of any decency is in short supply save for the short sharp bursts of Arctic wind that blows through when some of the airside marshalls go in and out of the door at the front.

At this point, it feels as if the airport and airline are collaborating to make your life as miserable as they possibly can. Their sadistic tendencies know that the only reason you're on this flight is because you have pretty much no choice. The success of your job relies on you being up at this time of day. So what do they do? They starve you of oxygen and heat to sap your energy levels completely. You'll be pretty much defenceless by the time you board the plane, thus rendering you incapable of any straight thought. You might even stretch to complimenting them such is your stupor!

Then there is the bus! Roops loved the bus the most because it throws all the jostling and barging that took place up to this point into the air (the only thing up in the air ironically). All that pushing and tactical manoeuvring to basically board a bus. So much wasted energy used up.

When stepping outside the terminal, usually into extremely cold air (airports always seem to be built in the very coldest parts of the country), you are sometimes presented with a choice of two, maybe even three buses. It's still 0630 in the morning, you're cold, miserable, bruised and basically incapable of applying rational thought to anything. And just like trying to pick which queue will be quickest in the Post Office, it's an absolute racing certainty that the bus you pick will be the slowest and last to make the journey to the plane. You can also guarantee that the position you take up on the bus will be precisely the place that ensures you're the last person to leave it.

The basic purpose of the bus is to cram as many people onto them as is humanly possible. It's not clear what the record number of people is but it must be close to 300 ... Roops firmly believed that the airport tarmac appeared to be in some strange No Man's Land, governed by their own rules, not needing to have to subscribe to the same Health and Safety laws as the rest of the land. Instead, they ensure that all you can literally see, smell and taste is the wet wool on the coat of the person next to you.

But vital in amongst this exercise is that absolutely nobody gets off the bus in the order in which they boarded. The bus pulls everyone from the front of the queue in the airport terminal and immediately turns them into the people who'll be last to get off - a trick that not even Paul Daniels in his pomp could have pulled off.

This means that the people that didn't give a fuck about boarding quickly are now at the front - continuing with this similar state of mind when walking up the steps to the aircraft and getting on to the plane.

They saunter up the steps, in absolutely no rush, to get on the plane, in absolutely no rush, to then take off their several layers of clothing, in absolutely no rush, turn and smile nicely at the assembled queue behind them, in absolutely no rush, as they carefully decide which precise part of the overhead locker they want to place their eight bulging bags, in absolutely no rush.

Meanwhile of course, and it is this in particular that Roops thinks is priceless, those who had fought so hard to get their place at the front of the queue are now left standing at the foot of the plane steps fighting an inevitable force 7 wind with some sleet thrown in for good measure. By the time they finally get on the plane, they look like a Hanna-Barbara cartoon character who has been standing in a snow storm with their hair frozen skywards and clothes dishevelled.

Now for Roops, this scene is only saved if he is boarding a reasonably nice aircraft – the Embraer 190 is his personal favourite for the flight to London City for example.

Larger aircrafts that go to Gatwick or Heathrow are quite pleasant too – however they usually carry holidaymakers which introduces all sorts of poor etiquette. Roops always tried to avoid flights to "holiday" airports because the people on the planes don't really know how to behave in airports and they're even worse on planes. He quoted it to a first time golfer playing at St Andrews; they just don't know the drill and the rules they're meant to follow, whether written down or not.

The type of plane that takes you to your destination therefore makes a difference and Roops had always been categorical in his wishes when explaining this to his PA. There was a certain order of events when booking travel.

First, try to get a flight to City airport with an airline which operates an Embraer 190. If a seat isn't available at the right price, look at other options such as Heathrow flights, or Stansted or even Luton.

Always, always, always, concentrate though. Whatever you do, avoid any airline which operates a plane that needs propellers to get it into, and stay, in the air. This makes a difference.

If, for whatever reason, your PA happens to be having an "off day" or perhaps they're on holiday and someone else is booking for you, then your already shit start to the day is about to be compounded when you find yourself climbing the wobbly steps up and into a Dash 8 aircraft.

For Roops, this was hell. He had a growing dislike for flying and he particularly hated this make of aircraft.

Yes, he could hear the makers of, and airlines that used, the Dash 8 holding aloft the efficiency and the environmentally friendly impact that these aircraft have. In fact, if it had been sponsored by the Green Party, he wouldn't be at all surprised.

"That's absolutely fine" thought Roops, "we all want a cleaner planet. But to extend that point, if that's the measure of success, then why aren't we all using bikes or even hang gliders to get to London? Neither of these use any fuel and from a noise pollution perspective are virtually silent, apart from the occasional faint screams of the petrified hang glider person."

The Dash 8 is cramped, noisy, slow, too hot and most importantly, seems completely incompatible with the UK weather systems. The wee thing seems to suffer from the most dreadful nebula-phobia which to Roops's mind, is always going to be a bit of a problem for something that basically needs to fly through clouds.

The slightest wisp of cloud over London City and this thing simply refuses to move. It goes on strike – it's the aircraft equivalent of 1970s' British Leyland. The only thing that's missing is a burning brazier surrounded by men wearing donkey jackets.

Roops got more and more exasperated by this. "The success of our economy is inextricably linked to the mood of an aircraft and it's apparent fear of flying in anything other than a clear blue sky," he would think as he sat yet again, on the tarmac listening to the Captain's reasons for why you weren't in the sky.

Now add to this how slow the thing is. It seems reasonable for most people to think that within the UK, you should basically be able to get to most major cities in around about an hour. Of course, at times you get delays, or are held up by congestion but in the main, you fly to most places in around about an hour.

If you get on a plane in the UK and are in the air for around two hours, Roops would expect with some good reason that when he first stepped off it at the other end, he'd be immediately hit with a wall of warm air and greeted with a cheery "Hola" or "Bonjour". But not if you're on a Dash 8.

This seems to trundle down to London via the most circuitous of routes to sneek the total travel time to a smidgen under two hours … which is an incredible feat when you consider that Edinburgh to London is all downhill! Gravity at the very least should have been a supporting factor.

Roops was convinced on one occasion he looked out of the window and was surveying the west coast of Ireland … so not only was the plane scared of clouds, it didn't do "flying in straight lines".

In addition to the apparently never-ending travel time, Roops hated the inside of the Dash 8 cabin.

In most normal aircraft – particularly those that charge you c£150 to fly in them – you get proper seats to sit in. Now admittedly the Dash 8 does have two lines of things resembling seats however they are probably only of a size which would comfortably accommodate a group of 5 year olds.

Roops though is a full grown adult and like many businessmen doesn't necessarily live the most healthy of lifestyles - unfortunately he has a backside which is testament to this.

The seats are thin, hard and completely unsuited to sitting in for anything longer than an hour - which would normally get you to most places in the UK, if it weren't for the fact that this was a Dash 8.

But bottoms, bizarrely aren't the arse of the issue. It's shoulders. You see the curvature of the aircraft is such that any normal sized person taller than 5 foot 10 inches and with standard sized shoulders, has to hunch or lean to one side meaning they basically have to take the flight sitting at an angle.

If the chap at the window is of any reasonable size then naturally he needs to take up some of the space of his fellow passenger, which is never pleasant for either of you. But at least trying to steal space on the armrest becomes child's play in that scenario.

And you're like this for almost two hours … The upside is that you're not tempted to buy one of their coffees both because you can't get your hand into your pockets to retrieve your money and because you couldn't actually lift the cup to your lips without the potential for third degree burns for you and your new Siamese twin.

Roops was conflicted. Whilst he quite liked the fact that someone had thought about building a plane that was being nice to the planet, and someone else in turn thought it would be good to buy a plane that was nice to the planet, he hated it.

As he sat there, all hunched up, only able to use one hand on his phone Roops felt he should compose an email to the people who design and make the Dash 8 aircraft.

"Dear Sir or Madam,

I'm a fairly regular traveller on aeroplanes, mostly domestically within the UK. Being a business traveller is not without its challenges – indeed I could probably write a book about it – however there is generally one period of the travel experience which represents a time of calm and even perhaps, solitude. That is, the time that you're in the air.

I have flown with most airlines around the country and enjoy the experience of the Boeings, the Airbus and I particularly like the Embraer 190.

However, from time to time, I need to fly on the Dash 8 and, well how can I put this?

Have you ever really looked forward to a big football match? The build up of the match that starts a week in advance, the manager interviews, the player updates, who's injured, who's in form, who's fallen out with the manager, who's wife is wearing the latest Prada, what this will mean to world rankings, reading the various newspaper analysis and the pundits speculating on formations.

Your anticipation is built up like a lovely froth on top of the loveliest of foaming frothing things.

You rush home from work ready to claim your space on the settee, beer nicely chilled, crisps and nuts near to hand. You plump up the cushion, move the cat, put your feet up. You lift the remote control and then you discover ... the match is on ITV. It's not on the BBC and it's not on Sky. It's on ITV ...

Those three letters just make your heart sink because it means you have to listen to Clive Tyldesley for the next 90 minutes.

That's what flying on a Dash 8 is like. It's the only polite way I can find to describe it. Your plane is the Clive Tyldesley of the aircraft industry - noisy, irritating and with an inability to get to the point quickly.

I'm really sorry – I know you made the plane with good intentions and I genuinely believe that you are trying to be very nice to the earth.

But your plane is called Clive and on really bad days when it's foggy, Andy Townsend is the captain ...

Yours faithfully,

Rupert X Wardhaugh "

Chapter 8
Strangers When We Meet

Rupert X Wardhaugh, in his mid-fifties, took a great pride in his appearance. He was "old school" in this respect - shoes always buffed to the point that he could see his own reflection, three maybe four different suits a week to allow them to rest between wearings, a crisp cutaway collar on a freshly ironed shirt and always with double-cuffs. He would avoid the type of cufflinks which could be regarded as "comic" but his ties would, whilst conservative, at least introduce some colour in an attempt to give away a little bit of personality.

Going to work without shaving was unthinkable and he had his whole morning process down to an art form. He would study closely every line on his face, every slight change in colour on his morning stubble keeping an unconscious diary of his ageing years.

More troubling for him was keeping a watchful eye on rogue hair growing from bizarre places at even more bizarre lengths. Ears and nose were obvious places that needed to be groomed regularly but eyebrows and the back of his neck similarly had an annoying habit of sprouting overnight shoots.

Apart from shaving, his teeth cleaning process was deliberate to the point of being on the verge of OCD. He would stare into his mirror, watching each deliberate movement left to right, back to front, concentrating on each tooth carefully before rounding off the process with some flossing and mouthwash. In all, together with his shaving, this took roughly 20 minutes. But to Roops, it was as much part of his uniform as his chalk striped suits and Church's brogues.

He couldn't begin to comprehend how someone could walk out of their door not having taken the same level of pride in their appearance. He knew, particularly in his role, that he was representing himself and his company. He was their public face before he had even started to speak - it was important that he gave people the right impression from the off.

When sitting in airports or standing in queues, he would observe his fellow man and woman, and he would see some who clearly worked at the opposite end of this spectrum to him. Roops found it incredible that people who shave every day – or at least stare at their face in some capacity every day – seem to either completely ignore small forests protruding from their nasal passages or worse, see it and think it's absolutely fine!

There are people walking around with what closely resemble the fingers of Chewbacca hanging from their nose apparently in the belief that they are on the cutting edge of a new fashion movement. And sometimes, these even carry stray bits of snot. It's just disgusting and to think that they're walking about in public!

Roops would sit astonished at this and secretly imagine setting up some new movement, leading the UK and appearing on The One Show to highlight the growing concern (no pun intended) of Britain's lack of self-control when it comes in particular to nasal hair.

"People of Britain" he would imagine himself saying, behind a lectern pictured with a clean nose. "We have reached crisis point. Nasal hair is not something we need to live with. You have a choice to trim, cut or pluck. Take control; make your choice! But for god's sake - tidy yourselves up!".

This short attempt at humour was his only light relief knowing that potentially he'd be sitting next to someone for the next hour or so who had the Forest of Arden coming from their nasal septum.

Roops would look with some sympathy at the passengers given their journey to this point. It was little wonder that by now, they just look like one long row of monochrome people – colour drained from their faces, completely pissed off with the world and probably close to some sort of self harm. He would compare the scene with the film about penguins which Morgan Freeman narrated which described the migration of the flocks in their search for food.

They looked like they'd had their life basically knocked out of them, trudging onto the plane all looking the same - completely miserable, beaten up by their experience, mostly indistinguishable from each other. With hair growing out of their noses …

There was always a sense of trepidation when Roops got on the plane – and a huge sense of hope – based upon the seating. He of course already knew in advance which seat number he had but it was highly unlikely that he knew where everyone else was sitting, introducing a huge game of chance.

Roops boarded with one thought and hope in his head – that is, that nobody would be sitting next to him. But that was always unlikely given that this is the first flight of the day, early in the week and the flight is usually rammed.

So in these circumstances, he hoped that the person who ended up next to him would be really attractive, a goddess even (like his wife). Someone who perhaps smells how he might imagine Princess Grace of Monaco would have smelled, with long flowing blonde hair, a wonderful smile and most importantly, saw him as the very most interesting person she had ever met.

Now that's all very well – however he'd had very little sleep, been pushed beyond the natural limits of irritation just to get where he is and was most likely about to spend the next hour or so dribbling into his crisp white collar to salvage his last moments of sleep.

What he didn't need was the added distraction of having to do all of this and still pull off trying to combine the sophistication and suaveness of the Sean Connery version of James Bond, with the wit and repartee of Peter Ustinov.

So whilst he acknowledged how unlikely it would be, he still got on the plane with one thought, one hope, namely "Fuck all that nonsense about a hot woman – I want both seats".

That's the ultimate prize. That's how bad things have become that he hoped and prayed that for the next 60 minutes, he could sit, spread out a little bit and not worry in the slightest about having to share space, air or time.

But really, the very best he could hope for is a seating partner who neither smelled nor impacted him in any way at all.

Assuming that he wasn't caught out by the bus moving him from the front of the queue to the back, Roops made it a mission to get to his seat early which allowed him the opportunity to claim an early bit of territory, even if it was just to claim the last piece of fresh air that he was going to be able to draw on for the next hour.

Roops sat down and listened to the Captain's welcome - the bit when he tells you the weather outside (you could have told him that - it was freezing), the weather at your destination (which will change by the time you land) and that at this point, there are no air traffic control issues (that too will almost certainly change). You're then told to "Sit back, relax and enjoy the flight".

Anyway, this gave Roops the chance to start to scan the collective faces of the boarding passengers as he began his game of "Please Yes/Please No" - that is, if you can't have both seats to yourself then each passenger is allotted either a "Please Yes" or "Please No" as they stumble up the centre of the cabin.

Although he wasn't some sort of psychologist or "people behaviourist", Roops did like to study people in all aspects. Their look, their mannerisms, even potentially their sense of humour.

Some, as they approached him, would courteously apologise that they're the anointed one designated to sit next to him.

"I'm sorry - I'm in 6A ..." they would say, sheepishly.

"Why are they apologising?" he would think, " you're now worrying me. What do they know about their travel habits that causes them to apologise in advance for whatever is about to happen?"

Roops would worry that perhaps they'd just been released from Broadmoor, previously held for crimes against someone who'd stolen their centre armrest. Maybe they were like one of the villains out of Scooby Doo and were hatching a plan to take over a nearby factory from seat 6A. If they were, they were at least very courteous about it.

Roops ultimate dread when playing his "Please Yes/Please No" game was that his eventual seating partner would be, well, overweight.

This isn't something that he'd say out loud or even in an open forum because it invites all sorts of accusations of discrimination. And let's face it, there are a lot of people who are overweight so it's best not to upset them. People get so sensitive about their weight and defensive if they've perhaps tipped the scales a bit too much over the Christmas period (or Easter period, or the holiday period, or in the winter months or even just over the weekend).

Being overweight isn't something to be laughed at, especially as it's very often combined with serious health problems whether they are physical or mental. Roops offered his utmost sympathy and he wished them nothing but good.

But similarly, it has to be acknowledged that some people just have appalling self-control and find it impossible to walk past a fridge …

Either way, serious weight problems can result in big problems when using public transport which is short on personal space. Compromise has to work both ways - that's what the word basically means.

It wasn't that he was being rude, but when finding himself in the situation of having a large person next to him, Roops would sit and stare at his ticket. Not because he was embarrassed to look at the person in the eye, but instead to double check that he was in fact entitled to one whole seat.

Not one and a half seats nor just one half of a seat.

"No, I'm definitely entitled to exactly one whole seat," he would think to himself. "It says it right here on my boarding pass - seat 6B, not a little corner of 6B, or half of 6B. I'm meant to get the whole of 6B. No dispute then."

"When I die," Roops thought, "I'm expecting my coffin to be just for me. Nice as it would be to have a bit of company on my final journey, it'll definitely just be me in there. Similarly, when I go to the toilet, I have a full expectation that it's a place just designed for me and me alone."

Some things are designed to be for one person only.

And in Roops's mind, this also extends to an aircraft especially when he's paid a few hundred pounds for the pleasure. When he sits down on a plane, and knows that he's trapped on it for roughly an hour and a half in total, he expects a reasonable amount of personal space and that each person courteously respects it.

However, some people are so large that naturally they will spill out in all directions. They can't help doing it and Roops was convinced that they were probably as embarrassed as he was but … he felt very awkward to think about it but it didn't make him very happy.

Rubbing up against someone else is a sport best reserved for the bedroom. Or the kitchen if it's quiet. And sometimes the utility room. But a plane? Nah, that's just wrong - Roops didn't care what folklore says about certain clubs, a plane at this time of day is just for sitting on and not touching other people.

"There's something really horrible and creepy when sitting down on a flight (or anywhere) and your thighs rub against someone else's. It consumes you for the entire flight. When they flinch, you feel it. When they move slightly, it feels like you're moving a lot. You can't eat because you feel every chew they take of their food. When they drop food (which doesn't happen that often it would seem), it falls between you both and you're left spending the rest of the flight wondering whether it's rubbed into your suit trousers," he would say, visibly cringing.

Now to be fair to Roops, he did note to himself that this would be exactly the same if the person next to him was actually slim, but with two slim people together it's easier to observe this thing called "personal space". Personal space is the one sacred thing you can ask for and should expect when travelling - you don't need to smell someone's breath to hear what they're saying, you don't need to rub their legs to know they're there – you have eyes and ears that do all of that for you.

Roops wasn't advocating any particular action against people who are unfortunate enough to be overweight – he certainly wouldn't write an email to anyone about it. He was just feeling compromised that all sympathy seems to lie in one direction on this particular issue.

But he was on a roll now and building up quite a hatred for whoever it was that was about to sit next to him. Roops had already decided that whoever it was would most likely to be a pretty disgusting individual.

He didn't even reserve his ire for fat people. It is the same with really tall people too and especially their knees. He was really sorry that they can't sit without their legs touching their ears or at an angle of roughly 130 degrees but that wasn't Roops's fault. He just wanted them out of his personal space. Just thinking about it made him want to go for a quick shower.

Even if they were slim and relatively normal, he'd decided that they almost certainly wouldn't smell very nice. And this was a real bugbear of Roops's because personal hygiene is entirely within the control of every individual. Just like nasal hair.

"Is it really too much to expect from professional business people, who have presumably attained a certain level of education and status in life, to at least be familiar with the workings of a shower, toothpaste and deodorant?" he would moan. "Not to mention the benefits that a good wash brings to you and consequently the impression that the people in your immediate vicinity have of you?"

"Why do some people appear to have no knowledge of the fact that naturally, they smell awful and a little bit of artificial support would help them massively?"

So as Roops sat there, scanning all of his potential neighbours, the future really looked quite bleak. Granted, he wasn't on a holiday flight or on one of those Friday afternoon flights to Dublin where pretty much everyone on board is completely hammered and only show a passing regard for in-flight protocol. But the chances were that whoever it was, they were going to be pretty disagreeable in a number of ways.

So if he couldn't get the seat next to him to be empty, he hoped for a glamorous and fragrant Grace Kelly-like beauty. Failing that, a reasonably proportioned person who washed and groomed themselves would work. But if fate wanted to dump on his head from a great height, he'd get a 6 foot 7, 22 stone monster with hair coming out of every orifice.

As he sat there though, his very biggest nightmare presented itself in the form of a loud "Shriek!"

He'd been caught cold and couldn't defend himself properly against this. The one scenario that he really, really dreaded more than anything. This was worse than someone trumping in his face or sitting on the corner of his thigh.

His really biggest dread of all was that he was sat next to someone that he "sort of knew". And here they were.

"How cool! We're sitting next to each other!" this person from Roops's office screamed as Roops did his best impression of being nice whilst being massively pissed off at the same time. It's a face that takes some practice but unfortunately is so subtle, it requires the recipient to actually be concentrating on it at the time to appreciate what's going on.

Next to him was a person who he'd never spoken to before, but occasionally nodded at when he passed them on the office stairs or in the canteen. Someone he'd seen around, half knew their name and sort of had a faint idea of what they did. It was a relationship so devoid of any hard detail that he would never be considered a reliable witness in court if ever asked for any description of the person.

"Oh fucking hell" thought Roops, "they honestly believe that they have every right to hold a lucid conversation with me for the next hour. This is a living nightmare. I have absolutely no spare inane platitudes to share with this person. Oh Christ, what have I done to deserve this …?"

But to compound this, this was one of those people who travel so rarely that even the slightest hint that they recognise anyone at all, sends them into a level of excitement more akin to a seven year old child on Christmas Eve.

Roops just looked in shock at the person next to him, this grown adult who was now hyperventilating just because fortune has thrown them together on a plane to London.

Of course, it was too much for Roops to hope that his new plane partner knew "the rules". If they did, they surely would have merely have nodded at him, offered a polite welcome with a "yes I know you from the office" type of look and then let him get on with his journey in peace.

But no such luck. The travelling novice thought that he and Roops sitting next to each other is just the most amazing coincidence of luck and saw it as a message from a higher being that they should in fact be soul mates.

"Oh god, this is great. I'm so glad that I'm sat next to someone that I actually know! I hate these morning flights and I'm a bit of a nervous flyer. I just end up talking all the time."

"Mmm. The good fortune's all mine. And without being pedantic, I don't think we do actually know each other of course" Roops thought to himself. "I don't even know your name and I'm even struggling to work out your sex because you're shrieking at me like a small girl who's just been given a pony."

But his new friend continued reacting to this once-in-a-lifetime good fortune in a way not seen since someone told Sharon Osbourne that the public was remotely interested in anything she had to say.

Roops considered his options carefully:
1) Pretend to fall asleep – this is difficult if you're not actually that tired but you will be soon given the guy's determination to take you through their weekend, minute by minute
2) Dominate the conversation yourself with inane chat. This takes a lot of energy though as you have to do all the thinking and obviously talking. You also risk your own reputation; think of the person getting back to the office and telling everyone they meet just how incredibly boring you are at 0630 in the morning …

3) Fake a bad cold or another contagious disease – they won't want to look at you let alone breathe the same air as you.
4) Tell them you're a really nervous flyer and could you hold their hand and join you in prayer.

Roops instead just sat in seat 6B completely resigned to the fact that the law of averages dictated that he'd ended up sitting next to someone that he frankly couldn't stand. He had no other choice other than to get on with the job of just staring ahead at the seat in front of him for the next hour as he listened to the stream of consciousness coming at him from the person to his left.

Roops drifted off thinking about his recent travels, his working life, his career to date and his career going forward. Questioning himself at each point, his boredom letting him reminisce about the most futile and stupid things.

The plane is now in full "circling mode" which means that it would like to land, however the "no air traffic control issues" announcement at the start of the flight has turned out to be a complete lie once again. Roops knew it. The airport below is actually full to bursting and as such, the International flights get priority.

This wasted time staring at parts of Oxfordshire that he never wanted to see, allows Roops the time to compose a new email to the Head of the Airline Cabin Crew offering some thoughts on improving the overall experience. He had high hopes. High hopes that it might be read - clearly absolutely no hope that it would be taken seriously.

"Dear Sir or Madam,

For many years, I've sat on your planes watching everything that goes on. I can recite at will your safety demonstrations and Captain's welcome and in that respect, I'd imagine that I'm probably no different to most other regular travellers on the flight.

It occurred to me that although you have a requirement to tell us these things, very few of the people on board will get much value from being told to "sit back, relax and enjoy the flight". I don't want to piss on anybody's parade here, but we don't actually know how to "enjoy the flight". It's a completely meaningless statement.

Wilbur and Orville Wright used to enjoy their flights. I'm sure the pilot gets to enjoy his flight. But we're stuck in the back here next to people that we don't want to be next to and we're faced with lies about the weather being fine, the flight being on time and the food being edible.

So alongside the things that you have to say, I thought that you might want to start introducing a few new things to your routine which I think would really benefit me and my fellow passengers.

Bizarre as it might sound, but most people have already worked out how to fasten their seat belts. It's one of the easiest things in the world to work out.

But a teeth cleaning demonstration? That would be a fantastic idea. For some reason, the left/right, left/right movement of a toothbrush in their mouth seems to be too much for some, if the smell of their breath is anything to go by.

Similarly, rather than serving up hot breakfasts - which let's face it only serve to stink out the cabin both pre and post consumption - you could run a "facial manicure session". Most of your crew are impeccably presented and they could start sharing their beauty secrets, the first "secret" apparently being that the hair which grows out of your nose is ugly but can be trimmed.

We Business Travellers are pampered, middle class, mostly overweight people who have spent the last hour gorging on croissants, toast and muesli in the Lounge. If we haven't, then that's our fault for not getting up early enough.

So please don't feel compelled to both add to our collective girth and to the increasing levels of food waste that blights our land (and skies) by filling us with warmed up bacon and rubber egg. Instead do some real good and make a positive difference to your passengers.

Yours faithfully

Rupert X Wardhaugh

p.s You can support my "Campaign for the Reduction of Free-flowing Nasal and Ear Hair" on Twitter: @Freethesnotandwax."

Chapter 9
Station to Station

The plane landing, and by that, when its wheels physically touch the tarmac introduces the modern day ritual - or First World experience - of mass beeping and bleeping around the cabin as every electronic device reconnects with the world. Roops was no different and he himself had both his work phone and a personal one to contend with.

Most of the emails that arrived whilst he was up in the air were the usual bland overnight range of adverts and circulars so Roops re-read some of those that he'd flicked through when he was back in the Departure Lounge.

One jumped out at him - or to be more precise, the content of one jumped out at him more than most. Why hadn't he noticed this before? He stared down at his phone in disbelief at what he was seeing.

Earlier in the morning, he hadn't really bothered to read closely what he thought was a fairly standard email about his travel arrangements for the following weeks - he just opened it because he had time to kill whilst the plane taxied to the terminal. It was a the standard banal email from his PA detailing his travel times and which hotels he was booked into. Or it should have been.

But now that he was a little more awake, something jumped off the screen at him. Something didn't look right.

The times didn't marry up.

"How on earth can I be taking off at 0630 and not landing until 1100? Not even FlyBe can take that long to get to London??" he was thinking. "The travel company have outdone themselves this time".

He stared at the departure time again and then the arrival time, checked the dates, checked that he was actually arriving in London and not New York ... then with a shattering blow, he saw one damning piece of information.

He wasn't departing from Edinburgh airport - he was leaving from Edinburgh Waverley. He was booked on the train.

Next to it though was even worse news. He had a fellow passenger with him - Mr J Sylvester.

"What the fuck is going on here?" he muttered to himself.

Roops scrolled furiously through all the other "bland emails that he hadn't bothered reading" to find one that might give him some insight to this piece of news. It wasn't too unusual for there to have been a lot of email traffic throughout the evening given the ability his colleagues had for whiling away the hours of an empty night arguing with each other and copying everyone else in for entertainment. Last night had been no different.

Finally though, one note stood out from the rest.

"There you are" he said as he spotted a note from his boss, Trevor.

He never really got on with Trevor as neither in fact, had he ever really got on with anyone who was regarded as being in authority or "managing" him. Roops liked to work alone, proud of his own work ethic and understanding of what he was meant to do. But Trevor more than most wound him up.

Trevor is an actuary, not that this alone meant that Roops couldn't quite take to him but it was undoubtedly a contributing factor. An actuary is a scientist of numbers, someone who might see something work in practise, but won't believe that it's true until they can prove that it should also be able to work in theory.

Roops would often wind Trevor up on this point and probably most other points relating to his profession too.

"When you went to Actuary School," he'd start "did you all get special dictionaries with the word "pragmatism" removed on the basis that you'd never ever need to know the definition of it?"

"Yeah, good one. Spot on." said Trevor.

"Did they also offer fashion and social behaviour advice to you at Actuary School Trevor?"

"No, of course not ..." Trevor would respond sniffily.

"Thought not! Obvious really!" Roops would throw back, laughing heartily.

"Yes, yes, very good," Trevor would reply wearily. "I really have heard all these before Roops. They also taught me complete disdain at Actuary School too - I got a First in it. Just you stick to Relationship Management ..."

Trevor was the sort of person who had never really embraced social skills, speaking his mind without apparently any appreciation of the impact his opinions would have on anyone around him. Although he had an IQ numbered so high that most people would have fallen asleep before they counted it, he conversely had an EQ which barely crept into single figures, such were his problems when interacting and relating to others. This

94

had nothing at all to do with him being an actuary - he just had very poor social skills!

It was a strange quirk of his industry he observed - pack the leadership full of technicians at the expense of people with whom their customer base could actually relate to on a day to day basis. And vice versa.

Of course, the irony of Trevor having oversight of a relationship management function was never lost on Roops. Never ever. Never ever when Roops had to have monthly one to one's to talk about managing people and relationships to someone who thought the world should work off a spreadsheet.

It was the hardest meeting of the month, particularly when Trevor had the audacity to offer advice on "how to handle particular situations" quoting phrases from some management book he'd recently speed read during a shit break.

With considerable trepidation, Roops opened the note from Trevor.

"Hi Roops, hope you're well - I'm just following up on what I was mentioning to you the other day.

I've been thinking it would be a good idea for you to help develop Jamie Sylvester. I don't think we're using him properly and getting the best from him. He's really impressed me recently with his work on Project Antelope.

I know you're planning to see the new account next week so I've asked Sandra to book the two of you train tickets to go down together. That'll give you time to go over a few things with him.

I know how much you enjoy the train.

Cheers
T"

Roops felt like throwing up. Not only was his boss now booking his travel he was imposing a trainee on him, the overly enthusiastic and chipper Jamie Sylvester. This would be unbearable. And when exactly had he "mentioned" anything close to this other day?

And what's this about getting the train?? The train!!!

Now Roops was a master at complaining about airports. He considered himself arrogantly to be considerably more knowledgeable on the topic than anyone given he spent most of his life in them. But for all the hassles and irritations he faced at airports, he would always vote for flying over getting a train to London any day of the week.

He was getting really, really bored with this ongoing debate around whether the train is in fact better than a plane.

It was a debate he'd often had with Trevor when going over his expenses. It was a futile debate for Roops, like the "you say tomato, I say tomato" argument or the "is it Bowie (the proper Scottish pronunciation) or Bowie (like an American)".

"Trevor, you're only saying the train is better because you've set up a spreadsheet to work it out," he'd say. "I'll bet you're taking into account the total travel time, divided by a frustration factor and multiplied the answer by a probability of delay. Then you'll have added a quotient to balance off the food on offer and the fact that there is no hassle with bottles of liquid which are over 100mls!"

"If only life could be calculated like that" argued back Trevor, "it would sort some of your daft theories out Roops!"

"This is just like your Chrysler argument Trevor," countered Roops.

The Chrysler argument was a well trodden path between the two of them. Trevor rhyming off fuel economy stats, the reduced road tax, the load of extras that come as "standard" or the final, nail in the coffin, "you're not winning this argument" genius line - "it has 5 years of free servicing".

"But Trevor, at some point you'll have to sell the thing. So not only do you have to put up with the humiliation of driving a Chrysler around for 5 years just to maximise the benefit of all these goodies, you're also unlikely to find another fool who'll then buy it off you. This means you'll probably lose money on the resale value when you finally decide to purchase an Audi. Which is what you should have bought all along!"

This argument had raged for some time. Since the day in fact that Trevor announced that he'd just bought a Chrysler.

Their latest debate regarding the train came only last week. It followed a familiar routine, beginning with some gentle joshing like a little game of ping pong, each side taking their turn to slowly wind the other person up.

This time though, it had some added spice as Roops had come more prepared than ever. He'd realised that it was quite easy to distract Trevor with philosophical debates like this which meant he then never focused too hard on work matters. For Roops, this was the ideal outcome - getting through yet another monthly one-to-one with Trevor without actually talking about his work.

So on this day, Trevor started by trotting out lots of reasons as to why he saw the train as a better mode of transport over a plane. Roops sat back, stared at the ceiling and listened intently to the rapid-fire stand-up routine coming from Trevor, with the ironic rhythm and regularity of a train hurtling down a track.

In some respects, Trevor's arguments were just too rehearsed, too polished.

He'd cover:
- the "fact" that there's reduced security;
- the "fact" that the train takes you into the centre of the city;
- the "fact" that you can "get work done" on the train;
- the "fact" that there's great WiFi;
- the "fact" that you can make phone calls;
- the "fact" that First Class is actually cheap on a relative basis;
- the "fact" that you get an endless supply of drink and food;
- the "fact" that it's just as fast as the plane;

"This is the true mark of someone who doesn't believe themselves what they're saying" Roops would say.

"You're over explaining your points and people can see through that. This has come because you've had 6 hours sitting in one seat with nothing else to do other than stare at trees, whilst you tried to convince yourself that being on the train was a great idea, when in actual fact a voice in your head is screaming "Why hadn't you just flown to City!!"".

"Chrysler, Chrysler, Chrysler is all I can say" retorted Roops. "And since when did they teach monologues at actuarial school?"

There was no way on this earth that Roops was ever going to concede on any point in this argument, although as a tactic, it always helped to at least give the illusion of a concession being made. He always did this at the start.

Roops was slowly getting wound up though as Trevor droned on. He waited impatiently on an appropriate time to interrupt.

"Yes, but ..."
"Uh-huh but ..."
"Yip, yip, yes ... but ..."

Finally, a pause for breath comes from Trevor and Roops leapt. He wasn't giving any ground back.

"Right, yes, now - to my mind Trevor" as he started his equally well-rehearsed and structured defence "there are two very strong reasons for using the train over the plane."

Trevor looked surprised. "You mean you're saying that sometimes the train is better than the plane Roops? Are you finally seeing some sense?"

"Just hear me out," said Roops. "So to start again, there are probably only two very strong reasons for using the train over the plane."

"You said probably ..." interrupted Trevor.

"What?"

"The first time, you said "two very strong reasons" and the second time you said "probably two very strong reasons ..." said Trevor glowing with triumph.

"Anyway," continued Roops glowering at Trevor "there are two *very* strong reasons for using the train over a plane.

These are:

1) If something bad is going to happen it's indisputable that you're probably better off being on a train that breaks down than being on a plane that breaks down. Being on a plane that suddenly stops working properly does feel as if it's likely to be a whole lot more painful. And you're likely to be scattered over a wider area – so it's messier for those who have to clean you up afterwards.

2) You don't need to queue through lines and lines of security to get on a train – you simply walk on which of course, creates a mental conflict. Which is why I said "probably". Although I hate the security queues and the complete lack of any sort of process at airports, they do have the benefit of stopping people who want to blow up your plane, or who might want to shoot you, from getting in. A train can't offer you that level of comfort. Basically any nutter (with a valid ticket for the time of that train) can get on and do what they want."

"So there you are. Two reasons why you're probably better on the train - and that's the only two concessions I'm going to give you on the positive side for a train. There are however, many things that work against trains over planes …"

"Firstly, train stations are generally outdoors which means that even in the height of summer, they're freezing cold. Bitterly, bitterly cold. They have an uncanny habit of being positioned so that even the faintest puff of wind is somehow turned into a blast close to an arctic gale. No amount of goose-like down is going to protect you."

"Yeah but what about in summer" interrupted Trevor.

"Trevor, I already mentioned that. We live in Scotland. We only get one day of summer a year if we're lucky and even then, only in leap years ..."

"Now I've been giving this next reason a lot of thought. You need to concentrate but it's worth it. You might even thank me for pointing it out ..."

"Airports will tend to fly planes to destinations like London, Miami, Rome, Paris, Los Angeles - glamorous foreign resorts. On the other hand, they also fly to regional Hubs which in turn will fly holidaymakers on to said glamorous places. As a result, the people at airports tend to be people who want to go to places like that or indeed, need to go to these places for business. They are a certain sort of person in other words."

"OK ..." cringed Trevor.

"The train is a bit different. Take for example, the Edinburgh to Helensburgh route which on paper sounds a beautiful journey. Two wonderful places at either side of Scotland both famed for their beauty and general bonhomie I think you'll agree?"

"You could dream of travelling through beautiful green countryside, sipping champagne or having afternoon tea with cakes and scones whilst "the train takes the strain". It sounds idyllic doesn't it?"

"The problem you have with this journey though are all the bits in between. To get from Edinburgh to Helensburgh, the train passes through such salubrious areas as Uphall, Bathgate, Armadale, Airdrie, Easterhouse (bloody hell – Easterhouse!), Shettleston, Glasgow, Partick, Dumbarton ... if you don't get the idea - these are not places that you'd necessarily want to stop by and visit. Even if you were Ross Kemp planning another Sky 1 show, you would possibly pause for breath when approaching these towns but most probably you would just keep travelling on through when you saw their true horror!"

"You're such a snob Roops ..." interrupted Trevor ...

"Yes, and so are most people. Snobbery is merely a description of people who don't share your views or of people who share the views that you're not prepared to admit to in public. But that's a different debate Trevor" said Roops, holding his hand up in an effort to avoid heading off into one of Trevor's famous tangents. "No Roops, I have to protest! You're forever complaining about holidaymakers at the airports! This is no different ...!". Trevor laughed, exasperated.

"You're right, but for the purposes of this argument, that's irrelevant. Now, let me continue."

"The reason that the train stops at these places is because the train has to serve all of these stations in between. This means that not everyone who gets on this train actually wants to go all the way to Helensburgh nor are they on the train just to enjoy a gentle day tootling across the country."

"Statistically in fact, (Roops knew that because Trevor was an actuary, he was emotionally programmed to concede as fact any statement that began with the word "statistically") most people on the train actually want, or more probably need, to go to one of the places in between. Multiply this by all the other trains leaving your station and passing through all the little towns "in between" and very quickly you can build a social demographic of just about every town you never wanted to visit."

Even Roops was a little embarrassed by saying this out loud but he knew this theory to be true. He never, ever, wanted to go to

Armadale or Easterhouse. That was just a fact. He'd seen them on a documentary and decided there and then that his life could be in no way improved by visiting them. His life could potentially end very quickly, he thought, but not improved.

He continued his case to Trevor by quoting a new found love of theoretical and hypothetical statistics.

"All of this means that roughly 90% of the people in the train station look as if they want to stab you. To back this theory up, every twenty minutes there is an announcement over the PA system saying "This station is being constantly monitored on CCTV". Now why would they do that if they didn't think something bad could happen?"

"It's like walking into the modern day equivalent of 70s downtown Bronx. Last time I was there, I was expecting to see Starsky & Hutch getting their shoes shined by Huggy Bear in the corner of the ticket hall. I should have suspected something when the ticket inspector was wearing a UN Peacekeeper's helmet ..."

The ice like structure of Trevor's face cracked at this point. "Roops, you do realise that with statements like that, you're just undermining your own argument? That's just outlandish!"

Undeterred, Roops continued "So the station is like something from an old World War 2 movie in Eastern Europe – freezing cold and full of people you wouldn't really want to associate too closely with."

"And whilst there are faint attempts at introducing some luxury, they just can't help appealing to the better nature of the majority of their constituents. Take the bars for example. Once upon a time they were named after eras harking back to the "Golden Age of Steam" – The Rocket, The Flying Scotsman, even The Mallard –

eliciting a vision of ginger beer and cucumber sandwiches, sunny days on the beach and paddling in the sea."

"Now, they just get straight to the point and name the pubs things like "The Beer House". This needs no explanation or marketing. It's no nonsense, down and dirty - "We know you'll never come in here if you think we're a bird sanctuary. We sell beer from 5am. Fill your boots" should be their strapline."

"In case this needs underlining, this does not create an ideal scenario. It does not make the train station an attractive, warm and welcoming place to be. It feels dangerous."

"Right, ok" interjected Trevor. "You might have a point, but that's just getting on the train. If you time it correctly, you don't need to linger in the station so all of that means nothing. And in your two opening concessions, you missed a third - you can get some work done".

Roops just about spontaneously combusted.

"God, I hate it when I hear that. I'm just left absolutely speechless when this is trotted out! I mean Trevor! You're meant to be an intellect."

"If people really, really need to "get some work done" why on earth are they travelling anywhere in the first place? Why aren't they staying in their office if their work is so important to them?"

"If, on the other hand, they need to travel to "do work" then wouldn't it be better to get to their actual intended destination more quickly? Presumably the whole act of not working in their normal location is because there is a need for them to go to a different place to "do work"?"

"I personally want to get my travelling over and done with as quickly as possible so that I can get to my destination precisely to "get my work done". If I need time to read something or, as it's traditionally called, prepare, I set some time out in my diary in advance to do this …"

"Now, I'll be kind and assume that what you might mean is that you can spend time writing things or reading things and using the travel time efficiently. But when I hear that, I think what you're really doing is filling the hours and hours of boredom by reading and writing things. You're actually saying "I read and write to stop me from going mad having nothing to do but stare at trees for five hours.""

"And I hate to point this out - and without wanting to piss on your parade here - planes let you read things and write things too!"

"OK, granted if you fly, you don't get as long to read and write things– generally one hour versus four and a half from Edinburgh to London. But that shouldn't be taken as a negative - it merely means that you arrive at your destination more quickly which gives you more time to do what you actually set out to do in the first place which is your work …or am I missing something?"

"Even if you get the very first plane versus the very first train you generally get at least an hour and half more time in your London office by taking the plane. That's at least one extra meeting or even one and a half hours to "get some work done" within an environment where you're not relying on a spurious WiFi connection that makes you go through innumerable security questions every time you click Safari!"

Trevor just shrugged in defeat. But Roops wasn't finished

"And there's more ... The thing with planes is that mostly they come in a fairly standard shape. Rows are numbered from one at the front gradually increasing until you reach the back of the plane. It never really changes (as far as I've seen anyway)."

"Seats are generally A to D or A to F depending upon the configuration. This means that when you want to book a precise seat, it's fairly easy to work out where you'll end up."

"Trains on the other hand have the most mystifying seat configuration ever known. It's been designed by some weird algorithm which even you, Trevor, with your case full of spreadsheets would struggle with."

"The last time I sat on a train, I had a single seat numbered 5. The seat in front of me was number 11 and the seats across from me were numbered 9 and 15 ... I kid you not. How the fuck do they get that? It just doesn't work nor make the blindest bit of sense!"

"All of this means that booking a seat is an enormous game of chance. Booking on well known discount sites makes it nearly impossible."

"They even rub it in by offering you the choice of an airline seat! Nobody actually knows what an airline seat actually is in this context, and the site just metaphorically laughs in your face probably because everybody hopes it's a single seat and goes for one of those ...!"

Trevor was cracking up by this point.

"But Roops. You're forgetting one other thing that trains have that planes don't ... They have the Sleeper ..." offered Trevor.

"You're right" said Roops to a startled Trevor. "And you're only proving my point further."

"Eh?" said Trevor, completely bemused. "Come on then. Bring it on."

"Trains have an outstanding opportunity open to them which could and should set them apart from every other form of travel and which for many a business traveller would be the perfect solution to everything. It could be the business travellers number 42 - to quote Hitchhiker's Guide." (Another feeble attempt at trying to speak in language that Trevor would relate to.)

"You're right that The Sleeper has the potential to be bliss - be in London one day and rather than having to go to a hotel room after a late meeting or evening dinner, you hop on board a train, fall into a cosy cabin, go to sleep and waken up back home all fresh for the day ahead."

"But the train companies have managed to cock this one up completely too."

"And isn't calling it The Sleeper the biggest oxymoron ever?? How come the word "sleep" is used so often in instances when precisely the opposite happens."

"Children persuade their parents to invite their friends over for "sleepovers" when exactly the opposite happens. Absolutely zero sleeping takes place for a full 12 hours meaning the entire household is snapping at each other over the slightest thing for several days afterwards. You are basically left with jet lag without any of the benefits of two weeks in the sun beforehand."

"The Sleeper is the same thing. It paints a romantic picture of leaving one city in the dead of night for you to then awaken the following morning in another. This, of course, is mostly complete and utter bollocks."

"You do end up in another city the following morning - that part is true."

"But the reality is that you are placed inside a small cabin which, if you were cattle, would have animal rights activists marching up and down the platform waving placards telling the world how wrong it was (until it got too cold for them of course)."

"These cabins are also like real life time machines. Roughly eight foot by four, going inside one takes you back to the days of the 1970s three day weeks, Harold Wilson's calamitous Governments, flared trousers and glam rock. The family car of choice was the Austin Marina and when footballers were always covered in mud, never wore shin guards and sported comb over haircuts. Scotland still qualified for major football tournaments and none of the other home nations did - in other words, the complete opposite of what happens now."

"And with your claustrophobia Trevor, you'd hate it. I'm surprised you're such a fan?? The walls of these cabins are still covered with rugged, old carpets like those that you'd find on the floors of social clubs, stained with pints of warm brown ale. You could probably strike a match on them if you were confident that nothing in there was flammable. The beds are plastic moulded hammocks with thin mattresses on top and a strange combination of a duvet/blanket thing."

"But perhaps the most damning indictment of their unsuitability for the modern day traveller is that there isn't a single plug to be found for mobile phones or tablets. At the end of a long day, your phone is likely to have roughly 15% of charge left at a time when you need and want it most. You're left staring at the horror as the charge reduces and seemingly accelerating towards zero with each minute."

"Oh come on Roops ..." laughed Trevor. "It's not all gloom - you do get a sink! That's a least a nod to luxury!"

"A sink" said Roops, deadpan. "If there is one absolute and simple guarantee in life it's that this sink has never, ever been used for its intended purpose. Not one bit of it. No way, Jose ..."

"You see if during the night, nature makes a call then you need to tiptoe down the main carriage to one of the communal lavatories. Given there's a chance that you'll have removed your shoes for the evening, this makes the trip slightly more fraught."

"There's very little chance, especially if fellow travellers have been preparing for their journey in The Beer House, that you're the first visitor to the lavatory that evening. Men are not best known for their aim at the best of times however introduce the rough and erratic swaying of a train and not even the steadiest nor heaviest flow is going to hit its target. That first step inside the small cubicle and each one thereafter introduces the danger of that dreaded feeling of dampness. When you get that feeling of cold as the wetness from the linoleum flooring gradually seeps through your sock finally touching your skin makes you want to throw up. Except you see that someone else has already beaten you to that too ..."

"The result is that there are more varieties of puddles than the top floor of an NCP carpark."

"Given that this whole process has hassle and disease written all over it, I would bet quite a lot of money that most people just whip the old fella out in their cabin and aim for the sink. One word of warning though, if you don't use the latch to hold up the lid of the sink you're in grave danger of losing your best friend altogether." Roops closed his eyes in mock pain at this point.

Trevor had to concede Roops's sense of drama if nothing else.

"So yes, Trevor, I daresay there is a place for the train. They don't get held up by fog, they don't have to answer to air traffic control and generally, they're a safer bet of not falling from the sky. But when someone starts regaling you with reasons why the train is better for so many reasons, I just pity them. I'm sorry - I just think it's an enormous wind up."

"Ha! Thanks Roops! Very entertaining as ever!!" laughed Trevor. "And well done, you've managed to use up the entire hour so we can't look at my spreadsheet …!"

Roops left convinced he'd won at last. For once, he reckoned he'd managed to get one over his mad boss. He was feeling particularly smug with life and sat back in his seat to take a moment.

The last time Roops did get the Sleeper, it left him infuriated with a cross between sleep deprivation and wet socks. To put his anger to bed (in the absence of anything else being put to bed), he had laid back in his crib to type out an email of complaint - more derision actually - to the Head of Sleeper Services.

"Dear Sir or Madam,

I'll keep this short as I only have 7% of charge left on my phone and you can't even provide me with a plug to charge it.

Any chance you could leave some toilet roll next to the "sink" – it would save your patrons from getting carpet burns off the wall or from using empty crisp bags like you would do with a dog.

Many thanks

Rupert X Wardhaugh"

Of course Roops hadn't won that argument at all. Trevor was about to have the last laugh by not only foisting Jamie Sylvester on him, offering Roops up as some surrogate godparent which Trevor knew he'd hate, but by also booking them both on the train for good measure. It was pure and utter spite but also one monumental joke for Trevor.

"An actuary playing a little joke - who'd have thought? I'll be getting de-frocked!" Trevor laughed to himself.

PART 2
THE LONDON BOYS

Chapter 10
Slow Burn

Jamie Sylvester had a pretty boring life - a fact even he found hard to dispute. It was mundane, fuelled by an enormous chip on his shoulder borne out of a strong sense of entitlement. And the problem with people who have a sense of entitlement is that unless others agree with you, you're unlikely to get anywhere.

As a wise person once said, when you're born the only thing that you're entitled to is fresh air - the rest you have to work for.

For three years now, Jamie had been working in the same environment, doing the same thing. If he was honest, he couldn't even really remember the latter part of year one, most of year two and now here he was in year three. He'd passed through them all without really thinking about them or his career or whether it was on track.

True, every monthly review or appraisal was broadly positive in terms of the job he was doing and as a result, he'd always ask the same thing - "When do I get promoted?". Never "How do I get promoted?" and not even "Why am I not getting promoted?" - but always "When".

And always, Pamela his boss would say something like "Whilst I admire your ambition Jamie, just asking for a promotion doesn't mean you automatically get it. If you're serious about a promotion, and serious about your career, I need to see something from you that says you deserve it. I need to see something that means I can trust you with more responsibility."

Jamie would sit there blankly.

"Look at it another way Jamie. I can say I'm incredibly beautiful. I might believe that statement and people close to me like my parents will probably be kind enough to support the theory. But let's face it, all evidence clearly points in the other direction. You saying you deserve a bigger role and your ability to do it is sort of a similar thing. But if it helps, the difference is that you have it within you to refocus and grow. I, on the other hand, am stuck with this face and these enormous hips. So think yourself lucky!"

It frustrated the hell out of Jamie because he always felt he was doing a good job - every review he'd been told that he was doing a good job. So why didn't that mean he should be trusted with a bigger job? He could train other people to be good at his current job - isn't that "leadership"??

When he'd discuss it at lunch or over beers, the others told him he was doing a good job and of course, as friends do, they backed it up with stories about how everyone in the higher roles - such as Pamela - was actually doing a really shit job and those down the pecking order could do so much better.

But that's just the way things are in big offices and the pub theories were rarely backed up with any sense of reality.

From time to time Jamie would see others come in, do a job and then be whisked off to what seemed a glamorous role elsewhere in the business. He'd occasionally see them in the staff canteen, laughing and looking like they were really enjoying life.

It used to really rile him and get his back up. A lot of them were the "Graduate Trainees" - kids hand picked from university and considered capable of running the company one day. A bit like newly qualified drivers being considered, with absolutely no experience, to be the next Lewis Hamilton or Ayrton Senna.

114

Jamie thought it was favouritism aligned to an old school or an attempt to tick some sort of diversity box - it certainly couldn't be anything to do with talent otherwise he'd surely be in the frame.

If the bus journey into work was good for anything, it was for unleashing the occasional epiphany on Jamie. Like the time he realised that betting apps on his phone meant he never had to enter a bookies again. Or completing his tax return in September meant it very rarely missed the 31st January deadline ...

Sitting in his favourite seat on the bus recently, Jamie had his latest one - and this was a humdinger. Unlike any other day where he usually started reading The Metro newspaper from the sports pages backwards, the paper he picked up today was already open at the business section and in particular, an article on career management.

"ARE YOU READY FOR YOUR NEXT JOB?" boomed the headline. "Top tips for restarting your career" goaded the sub-heading.

This at least piqued Jamie's interest.

After offering some fairly obvious pointers on how to impress your boss (basically don't piss them of too much, make them look good and make their life easy) the same article then offered several books which the reader, if still actually reading, might want to explore for some further help.

To be fair to Jamie, he'd always been a bit cynical about these books. Books about finding your cheese or talking about chimps. "Business crap" he'd always said.

But this article made him think a bit more.

"What's the worst that can happen? I might as well try something different" he thought. So on this particular day, he stayed on his bus for an extra stop getting off in the centre of town to head to the large book store.

Down in the basement of the store was the "Business" area, sat right alongside "Psychology" and then along a bit from "Gardening" … he couldn't really work out the link and why they all sat so close together. He didn't really care. (One day it might be obvious!)

In front of him was an absolute plethora of books from all sorts of people. Some he'd heard of - the usual range of autobiographies from self-made millionaires and billionaires, telling about their secrets to success. Others were from lesser known people but again, all offering the single key to unlocking the door to promotions and a career of pioneering success. Jamie had no idea where to start, he was more in the dark now than he'd ever been.

He started picking up books at random - Richard Branson; Mark McCormack; Douglas Bannatyne; Steve Jobs; "The Secrets of Google"; "How to Get a Job at Google"; "How to be the next Google"; "Seven Day MBA"; "Ten Day MBA"; It went on and on and on …

"Christ, where do I start?" Jamie thought to himself. He was completely confused.

He decided to go on instinct, knowing that there was a fair chance that his choice could be a terrible one but then, as one of the "Think Positively" books would have told him, it might not be. Doing nothing had a definite and completely guaranteed outcome so at least he knew that wasn't an option. Today was all about creating new rituals!

He picked up a couple of books. One about working your inner chimp and another about managing relationships. They'd be a decent start he thought and by buying two, he might double his chances of some success - that betting app had at least taught him some things …

"Just doing his job" was what Jamie had been being paid for. He was good at that and the company was rewarding him for it - but they weren't seeing any sign that he could actually move on and do a different job. That's the thing he needed to focus on now.

Reading the back cover of one of his new books offered him an immediate point of focus as he wandered back into his office - "Are you being interesting or are you interested?" it said.

"What on earth did that mean?" he pondered. "I'm not even sure which one is the right answer."

Jamie couldn't get this question out of his head all day. He was clearly distracted to the point of being very quiet at his desk, something highly unusual for him. He was usually the life and soul of the office, always offering a joke, a cheeky smile, a bit of "banter".

Today though, he seemed lost in thought. He couldn't get this statement, this challenge, out of his head. Round and round it went.

"Am I being interesting or am I being interested?"

For the first time in years, Jamie realised that he'd stopped asking questions about those around him and those he was dealing with on the phone. He'd stopped being curious. He'd stopped caring.

He'd actually stopped caring about them and as a result, he'd stopped caring about his career. He wasn't able to to make a difference. He knew people phoned and he knew people needed "stuff", but he'd never thought to find out "why" they needed stuff. It had just never occurred to him to ask anymore.

When he stopped being a "trainee", he thought that was the day that he should be considered ready to do his job. It had never occurred to him that he had to keep on learning. Like the newly qualified driver, it's only after passing the driving test that you really learn how to drive a car.

Jamie realised on that day that he'd stopped being effective and had turned into a journeyman without realising it.

It was time to change. He had to start making new rituals. He had to stop being how he used to be.

Jamie started by consciously asking more questions, more and more of them beginning with the word "Why?". He felt like the most curious of five year olds, always questioning and not being blunted by the social rules of adulthood which tell you to "just accept it and be polite."

He figured that if he could really understand what motivated people and their business, what it was that drove them to "do what they do", to be in business, he would at least stand a better chance of helping them and maybe even offering up some solutions.

But much more importantly for Jamie, he found an incredible new level of enthusiasm within himself for his job and his career. He was absolutely buzzing in fact. He could see a difference in the way he was thinking about his job. He was really interested in the people he was working with.

The key hadn't been about what he'd read - it was the fact that he'd read at all.

That was three months ago and already people around Jamie could see change and progress happening. He never expected this new approach to offer sudden improvement but he was at least encouraged that by managing himself he had a better and more positive influence on those around him. For the first time in years, Jamie was actually making a contribution.

His team manager, the perfectly bland but functional Pamela, pulled him aside one day. She'd noticed a new maturity to Jamie. She could see his improved focus, the drive within him to improve both himself and by consequence, those around him, the fact he was paying more attention and delivering what seemed like a constant stream of ideas. He'd become more than just a journeyman and had turned himself into an asset. She decided it was time to offer him a chance, he was ready to take on more. Importantly, she was now happy to back him, conscious he wasn't the risk he once was.

Pamela also reported into Trevor and at one of her regular monthly meetings brought up the idea that perhaps it was time to give Jamie a chance. Let him loose on the outside world. Not in a way that would potentially endanger the future of the business but at least reward him for his new sense of purpose. And, according to Pamela, it would offer the company a bit of security should some of the existing relationship management team ever leave or die off (which was probably a greater possibility from what she'd seen of their lifestyle!).

Trevor had always liked the spark of Jamie's personality but was also aware that he potentially lacked a bit of depth.

It was nice that he showed some enthusiasm, but did he really understand what was going on in the world or was he the sort that just accepted things for what they were? Pamela had been feeding Trevor exactly the same thoughts about Jamie but had noticed a change recently.

There was a difference to Jamie and she thought it was time to give him a chance.

Trevor took some time to think it through but as ever timing was everything. Fresh in his mind was the ridiculous one to one that he'd just had with Roops and the monologue of the never ending train journey.

"This might just be the answer to it all" said Trevor.

"Eh?" enquired Pamela "Are we having the same conversation Trevor?".

"No, we're probably not" laughed Trevor. "But I'm about to make someone's day!"

Trevor had a lot of respect for Roops. He would even go as far as to say he liked him. Trevor knew fine that the two of them came from completely different worlds and he knew that Roops would never really understand his perspective of the world. But this "creative tension", he felt, was no bad thing. After all, without differing opinions, how can you ever be sure to make the right decision, he thought.

But having sensed a bit of frustration from Roops the last time they met, Trevor felt it was maybe time to give him a new project to manage. A new project called "Jamie Sylvester" …

A previously unseen sense of humour swept across Trevor when he first thought of it - he knew that Roops's immediate reaction would be somewhere close to apoplectic rage and so where best to break the news than when Roops was at his most distant from the office. On a plane, roughly 400 miles away, first thing in the morning, completely pissed off with the world!

There isn't a management book that existed that said that was the right thing or the brave thing to do. "But fuck it," Trevor thought "Roops would be the first to pull a trick like that. I'm sure he'll see the funny side of it one day!"

Chapter 11
In the Heat of the Morning

"That fucking dickhead! What the fuck is this all about!" spat Roops when he read the note from Trevor, the plane trundling down the runway towards the terminal building.

"The fucking, fucking, spunking asshole dickhead! He really just doesn't get it.! Jesus Christ, he can't even do spiteful humour properly!" he seethed, struggling to create any reasonable formation of swear words.

Roops would never concede that Trevor's move was actually a stroke of genius. Certainly not today.

But if this was a football match, Trevor had just pulled on the 1970 Brazil World Cup top and was hurtling down the left wing like a youthful Rivelino, ready to cross to Pele to nod the ball home.

But for Roops, who was already getting irritated at every little thing, this just about sent him over the edge.

Roops had already allowed himself to be irritated by even more shenanigans on the plane so was in no mood to be receiving news like this.

His latest source of frustration was the captain of the plane who'd just so expertly navigated his way down to London.

You see, if you've ever needed surgery the chances are that afterwards, you've thanked the surgeon. Similarly, once you've been to the dentist or the doctor you're likely to turn and offer some polite gratitude for the work they've done. It's just what reasonable people do.

Equally common though is their response – they tend to be fairly self-effacing, humble, very professional and even mildly offended when saying, "I was only doing my job".

They trained for years to make a real difference, to cure people, to care for people, to progress medical science and to get a better understanding of illness. They didn't train all these years just so that they could receive your thanks. They were just doing their job. Sometimes their job involves saving lives or supporting people through life altering moments but fundamentally, it's seen by them as "just doing their job" and it doesn't require celebration.

Rescue workers heading off to earthquake stricken regions similarly don't look for thanks. They're just doing their job.

Heck, even John McLane in the Die Hard films was completely laid back after saving Western civilisation on at least three occasions. He leant back, chomped on a cigar, smiled and said "only doing my job – yippee kay ay".

But airlines seemed to take a different view of this. Certainly as far as Roops was concerned.

"People should be rewarded for the exceptional but for "just doing their job"? Really? Isn't it a bit embarrassing to expect some sort of celebration?" he would huff and puff.

And of course, when Roops was in a foul mood, his position on all things moved to a more extreme end of the spectrum. It was amplified.

"When things go as we asked or expected, whether it's a plane taking off on time, landing on time, arriving at the right destination, or in other words, does the job it was paid to do, the airline industry reacts with mild hysteria!" he would fume.

"It seems that "just doing their job" comes as a bit of a surprise to them and as a result, is worth shouting about from the rooftops! They even have the cheek to sometimes come across as quite smug and with such an air of superiority that you'd think this was a complete anomaly when all they were actually doing was sticking to their contract with you!"

"I'd hate playing these fuckers at sport if this is how they react to what in effect is a no scoring draw!" he snorted. "It's not as if they've won anything – they just didn't lose. But these guys want to decorate an open top bus, ride through the town centre amidst hordes of adoring fans and receive a civic reception! Christ, they're just doing their job!"

"If I demanded this just for doing my job, I'd be spending all week picking the ticker tape from my hair!"

The more Roops thought about it, the more it irritated him which of course, was way more than it ever should have. But thinking about it was all he had to do. Here he was sitting on a plane, taxiing to the terminal with not much else to do at that point, other than to observe everything that was going on around him.

And he was fizzing mad anyway so everything was turned up to "Level 22" by now.

To Roops, landing on time should be as much of a given as landing the plane safely but no, landing on time deserves an announcement and a back slap from the pilot! Some airlines even go as far as to record a message from someone who sounds like a leprechaun who then plays a celebratory tune on a bugle!

Just for doing their job!

Roops rarely travelled on the so-called budget airlines because his stress levels couldn't take it but the first time he heard this tootling jingle, he just about burst. He couldn't believe what he was hearing!

When he bought his ticket, he didn't say, "would you mind sort of arriving around 8am" or "do your best mate" – he chose that flight, on that airline, because they contracted with him to land at his airport of choice at the said time. He certainly didn't expect mass self-flagellation in the cockpit just for doing so!

And then of course, there came the the announcement from the Captain. His "Landing Speech".

Anyone who has ever been on a plane will have heard it. It generally goes along the lines of:

*"Hello everyone, this is your Captain. Welcome to London –
we've got you here bang on time (pause for fist pumping and high
fiving in the cockpit). Whatever your reason for travelling with us
today, we hope you have an enjoyable day and we hope to see you
again soon."*

All in very calm, mellifluous British tones, devoid of emotion and to be fair, occasionally based on fact. And Roops hated every word of it!

He absolutely roasted with anger when he heard it. It's all very well for the Captain, who really just wants you off his plane as quickly as possible to sit there sounding like Donald Sinden and thank you for the pleasure of letting him fly you to London.

"If he was thinking about the passenger at all," Roops thought, "and in particular thinking of the passenger's context, his speech might be altogether different."

This wasn't the first time that Roops had been riled by this - of course it wasn't. The last time had been when he was travelling on one of the aforementioned budget airlines when he was heading to a different airport. On that occasion, he had plenty of time on the train into London to channel his anger by scribbling down what he thought a more honest landing speech should sound like. It would, in his opinion, be closer to something like:

"Hello everyone, this is your Captain speaking.

In spite of the fact that you've already been up for roughly four hours and now likely to have suffered from a level of sleep deprivation which makes you dangerously close to being medically diagnosed as psychopaths, having survived the humiliation and degradation of trudging through the security hall in your socks, hurdled over holidaymakers just to avoid serious injury and having sat for the last hour or so listening to the inane conversation of the person next to you whilst avoiding their stale coffee smelling breath, I'm sorry to say that your race hasn't even begun.

You've just reached the starting line, your Base Camp.

My friends, even after everything that you've been through up to now, from this point on, you are now in effect, proper London Commuters. And that's really shit. It's actually worse than really shit.

In London, they have a transport infrastructure so bad that a plate of overcooked spaghetti looks to have more order and rigidity to it. People have been lost in this system for weeks and nobody seems to know or care particularly where they are. There is a timetable system more confusing than a Salvador Dali painting and don't ever, ever expect to get a seat between here and central London. And by the way, if you manage to get a whiff of fresh air at any point in your journey, gulp it as you would a glass of water in the Sahara.

Not only that, everything costs an absolute fortune. On a value for money basis, there are Russian gang leaders looking into the local economy for tips on profiteering and blatant exploitation of the innocent.

And lastly, before I sign off, I must remind you of one last final damning piece of news … we've just landed at Gatwick. I'm sorry."

To Roops, the stickler for accuracy and attention to detail, it would be so refreshing if for once, someone in an alleged position of authority could just be a little bit more honest and transparent about the reality everyone was about to face.

"Please stop thinking you're great just for landing on time. Please stop telling us to "relax, sit back and enjoy the flight" as if we're on the Orient Express with a tray of sandwiches and a pot of freshly brewed tea in front of us. None of us are choosing to be here. We're all grown ups and we all know that it's just crap."

Trevor had cleverly sent his bombshell note at a time when Roops was guaranteed to be in his very worst mood. And things weren't about to get much better. As more and more emails started popping into his Inbox, Roops could see one from Jamie Sylvester himself. He didn't even need to open the email to feel the enthusiasm seeping from it. This was Jamie's moment in the sun.

For years, Roops had suppressed Jamie's progression, keeping him at arm's length, pointing out the obvious areas of inexperience and naivety. Jamie genuinely thought that getting down to London to "see people and do deals" would be the peak of his career. Maybe it would be of course, but in reality, it should only be his starting point.

Up until this point, to Roops's mind, Jamie had shown very little capacity for thinking about "why" he would be meeting companies, the areas of leverage they had over him, the areas of leverage that his company had in return over them, how the relationship could potentially develop, what was it that his company were trying to achieve and the other one trying to achieve in return. What really motivated each party?

And in Roops's mind, this was fundamental. What could Jamie possibly expect to achieve without as a minimum, understanding the absolute basics of relationship management.

"Relationship management was not about "being nice to each other". That's actually the last thing it's about!" he would opine.

The fact that Jamie kept shouting out that it was one big jolly just confirmed to Roops that he simply wasn't cut out for the role.

And then of course there was Trevor. What on earth was he thinking about? He lived in this little bubble of spreadsheets, all IQ and no EQ, never appreciating the benefit of a relationship management team. He just thought he could use the team as a playground for the enthusiastic young pups where to his mind, they couldn't do too much damage. The only time he really appreciated the area was when the shit hit the fan and nobody else had the balls to go and mop up the mess. Of course, because the area did its job so well, issues rarely flared up - thus putting greater spotlight on its value to the business. The classic victim of its own success.

"And I've been up since 4am to take this shit" thought Roops, wandering off the plane bracing himself for opening up Jamie's email.

"Hi Roops, hope you've landed safely!

Don't know if Trevor has written to you yet but he's asked me to pick up this new relationship. He suggested that I could go down to London with you, and that you could maybe show me the ropes?

He says that you'd be the perfect teacher for me!

He's asked Trisha to book us on the train. Trevor said you loved the train and it would give you and me lots of time to chat about this new arrangement.

On a personal basis, I'd also really appreciate if you could give me some pointers.

If you have some time when you're down in London can I give you a call?

*Cheers
Jamie"*

"Mmm" thought Roops. "He sounds genuine enough but god, I could really do without hand-rearing him when I've got my own stuff to deal with. Bloody Trevor. Is this the start of one big "cost saving" exercise when my higher benefit package can be removed in favour of the smaller one of Jamie Sylvester?"

"How ironic would that be? My success at coaching Jamie directly correlated to the potential of my very own downfall."

Roops didn't reply immediately. If experience taught him one thing, it was that emails are best written slowly and without emotion. Stick only to facts, give no room for ammunition to be fired back and whatever you do, never, ever wind people up. Roops had done that too often in the past and it only ended up with him looking a complete and utter arse that everyone hated.

So Roops wandered off to the Docklands Light Railway in amongst the huge and growing throng of passengers who had also landed at London City Airport, from all points of Europe that morning.

"How am I going to play this one?" he pondered as he stood on the DLR, as it snaked its way into the centre of London. He had to keep his dignity, that was for sure. He couldn't come across as threatened, or annoyed, or even slightly pissed off which was going to be a huge challenge given that was exactly how he felt.

No, he would need to make sure that Jamie came through this respecting him and looking up to him. Roops decided therefore that he'd have to be Jamie's teacher.

"Jeez, what a thought" mused Roops, as the awful truth dawned on him "this is going to end up like The Karate Kid and I'm his bleeding Miyagi ..." before chuckling out loud thinking "I wonder if I could get him to do The Crane in the middle of the office ...?"

Chapter 12
Killing a Little Time

London City Airport was Roops's favourite airport. He would sit and talk about his theories on this to whoever would listen. It seems obvious to say this, but not all airports are the same particularly the ones around London. For a start, some don't feel especially close to London.

For example, when Roops had to fly to Stansted airport, he'd still need an "Express" train to get him to Liverpool Street Station. This "Express" train takes roughly 50 minutes which for context is like landing in Glasgow when you need to go to Edinburgh.

In other words, it's nowhere near your required destination so they seduce you with words like "Express" in the hope you don't notice that "they're not that near at all - but we do have a very fast train for you."

But having tried it once, Roops was far from convinced. In fact, it just annoyed him.

"Maybe they used the word "Express" because it doesn't stop at any stations along the way. If you want to name your service anything", Roops would say, "call it "Not stopping at towns you've never heard of to get you to London as quickly as this shit network will allow" - not as snappy but way closer to the truth!" he'd bark.

Stansted does have some benefits he would concede in that you're rarely held up by Air Traffic Control and it's generally (early in the morning) devoid of holidaymakers on your flight meaning it's a fairly smooth exit from the plane and into the terminal. And the train is relatively regular - just not "Express" - but the station is about 300m under ground and takes ages to get to.

But without giving it too much credit, he also noted that it's only served by "budget" airlines so by the time you've landed you're very possibly still bruised by the experience.

With monotony, Roops would say the same thing "These planes – the orange ones or those painted in blue and gold (with leprechaun trumpets playing from them) seem to positively hate their passengers! I've never been to the Bangkok Hilton but I reckon that even they are more fair-handed in the treatment of their "inmates" than some budget airlines!"

Heathrow on the other hand, thought Roops, is a fine airport. For a traditionalist like Roops, he thought of it like the Royal Family of airports, magisterial and full of ceremonial pomp. He didn't always like it or agree with how it treated him as a domestic flyer but there was no getting away from the fact that it's the centrepiece and flagship of the UK family of airports.

He thought that as a nation, we need it there to feel safe and comforted. Occasionally, like some members of the Royal Family, it can be a bit bloated and full of wind, oblivious to those around them and perhaps carrying a sense of entitlement.

But "By god, it's British through and through and we're proud of it!" he would think whenever his plane touched down at it.

He would get the same feeling of it when he saw it on the news, or on American TV shows when along with Big Ben, it's used to epitomise "England". In other words, you're proud of it whenever you're nowhere near it.

When Roops travels to Heathrow he'd be instantly shepherded along a glass tube and directed to the outside of the airport. And that's fine, because he can jump on the very efficient Heathrow Express - which actually is an Express, doesn't stop anywhere (other than some of the other Terminals) and most importantly, it gets to central London quite quickly.

The issue Roops has with Heathrow is getting the plane to land there. The very point that he needs Heathrow to work in his favour, it rarely does. What he needs is Heathrow to be completely reliable at allowing his plane to land when it intended to land. Not circling in the sky for seemingly hours on end.

"I have absolutely no desire to see the fields of Oxfordshire, over and over again in ever decreasing circles. Maybe one day for my 60th birthday or something, I'd pay for a local flying club to take me up in a little plane for this. But the fact that I don't even know if such a tour exists probably tells you everything you need to know about whether I have any real wish for such a thing."

No, domestic flights landing at Heathrow is when the Queen of all airports has its annus horribilis, its Mrs Simpson moment, its Fergie toe sucking scandal.

Roops hated its obvious social class structure. Heathrow is very hierarchical and if you're just a little Airbus A319 popping down from Edinburgh you're in no way competition for the mighty A380 or the Dreamliner, or even the granddaddy of them all, the Boeing 747.

Such planes have been crossing the Atlantic or over Europe all night to soar down with crashing noise across the M4 axis. Domestic planes have to wait. And wait. And wait. Circling and circling like demented brown bears padding round their pens in a local zoo.

Heathrow in this act is like the Queen swatting one of her underling servants (if she ever did or still does such things – let's pretend that it's more like Queen Elizabeth I in Blackadder just in case the current one doesn't).

So whilst Heathrow is a beacon of all things Britishness to the outside world, it can also be all that is bad about Britishness from the inside too – one large class struggle where you sit firmly at the bottom if you happen to be in the wrong type of plane coming from the wrong part of the world.

Roops's very favourite airport sits snugly on the east side of central London. If the truth be told, it's the only airport that can say it's actually in London – which is quite something. (It also appears in the titles of EastEnders giving it a slight cockney swagger).

London City Airport is the business traveller's dream airport primarily because it seems to, in the main, serve mostly business travellers. This means that the vast majority of people inside are of one kind. They have one motivation which is to get from A to B as quickly and as smoothly as possible and to support this, they have very little luggage to collect and cart around.

Roops loved the fact that its passengers are not interested in walking at a snail's pace, of weaving randomly from side to side nor lugging three large suitcases with pink ribbons tied to the handles to make them stand out from all of the other suitcases with pink ribbons on them.

You can land at City airport and be in the City of London in roughly 40 minutes door to door.

When boring anyone who would listen to him of his love for London City airport, Roops's favourite story was when he had been on the 0640 from Edinburgh and then sitting having coffee in St Katharine's Dock near Tower Bridge at 0755.

"When London City airport works, it works brilliantly" he would announce, "like the most brilliantly, of brilliantly oiled things. It's Robert Louis Stevenson and Isambard Kingdom Brunel all wrapped up in one! And that's brilliant."

Even the route into London is the best in Roops's mind primarily because he mostly had to work in the City. The DLR takes him straight into Bank with the only drawback against its equivalent over at Heathrow being that it does keep stopping.

It can be very crowded and it can be smelly and yes, Roops used to marvel at how mothers still managed to get onto a crowded train with 4 kids and a pushchair. But the DLR is mostly above ground meaning you can stare at your phone and the emails piling in from the office in a journey totalling barely 20 minutes.

That's when it works. Roops, being the curmudgeonly commuter, will rarely tell you stories of when things work. It's much more cathartic to tell you stories of when things don't work and his day is completely screwed up.

And that simply is the problem with London City Airport. When the airport doesn't work, it's an absolute nightmare. City airport can be quite polarised – it either works or it doesn't. There's rarely a halfway house.

Its big issue is that it's located too close to London and Canary Wharf meaning even the slightest whiff of fog imposes some sort of speed limit on the planes landing, if indeed they land at all. If you're unlucky enough to be flying on the Clive Tyldesley of planes – the Dash 8 – the chances are that one little cloud in the sky is likely to throw your day into complete chaos.

Roops, like most other regular travellers to City airport has invariably at one time or another landed at a completely different airport – most likely "London" Southend … yet another airport claiming to be in London but with as much relationship to it as the famous London Birmingham or the London Bristol airports.

Landing at completely the wrong airport when you've planned your day so meticulously is, as you might imagine, a pain in the arse. Roops would go mad when it happened. He would snort with the best of them as if he was a brute of a horse on the start line of The Grand National.

He would confidently in advance, have planned a meeting for 0930 only to find himself somewhere west of London joining the commuter race fighting his way through to his final destination, invariably very late, the day ruined before it even started.

But what would really get his goat was that whenever his plane was diverted to Southend, the airline was only ever obligated to take you to London City airport which by this point, is the very last place you want to be. You wanted to be at London City airport an hour ago, not now.

Right now you want to be in the centre of London.

So when an airline lands you at an airport that you didn't want to go to in the first place, the last thing you want is for them to compound the issue by then taking you to a place that you originally needed to go to but which no longer has any use to you.

Roops would often say that it was like being in a big real life game of snakes and ladders. And you keep landing on a snake.

Today, thankfully, was a good day with City airport working like a dream which was at least one high point given the catastrophes (in his mind) Roops had already faced that morning. And now he had to give some thought about his forthcoming babysitting exercise with Jamie Sylvester.

Chapter 13
This Is Not America

Two weeks had now passed since receiving "that" email from Trevor and Roops had spent the intervening period both trying to suppress the enthusiasm of Jamie and at the same time, suppress his own dread for the trip.

But here he was now, the day finally upon him where he was going to have to grit his teeth and spend some intimate quality time, one to one with Jamie. Roops had been positively loathing this moment. He sat in silence in the rear of his taxi as he headed to the train station. Even asking the driver to take him to the train station gave him "the dry boak" (as his grandmother used to so eloquently put it).

Normally, whilst battling every other human and obstacle that the travel companies would lay at his feet, he at least had the comfort that he was entirely responsible for himself. He was left to his own thoughts and demons.

The anger and frustration of travelling acted as a sort of catharsis allowing him to be completely relaxed for when he had to do his job. Up to the point in the day when he had to do his job, he had mostly remained quiet although simmering with a steady rage at everyone around him. In other words, do precisely the opposite of what he was paid to do during the day whilst representing his company.

Since Roops needed to talk lots in meetings or give the occasional presentation, he needed to preserve his energy and even his voice in advance to give himself the best chance. So the obvious time to do this was when travelling.

Today though, he would have a travel companion. The young, energetic Jamie Sylvester who had been building up to this trip like an excited schoolchild about to take his first holiday away from his parents.

Every thought about the trip that entered Jamie's head in the run up to this, every morsel of consciousness that slithered from his being, seemed to immediately be put down in an email and fired across to Roops. This meant sometimes at least four or five times a day.

Roops started to wonder whether he could get his PA to see whether she could "accidentally" book them seats in completely different carriages on the train but he knew that Jamie's tenacity would only serve to cause more problems and in any case, someone was sure to find out and Jamie would be offended, and Trevor would get annoyed …

The plan was that they were getting the 0540 train from Edinburgh to London. Although it left earlier than most planes, it did have the advantage that they didn't need to go through security and this particular train only stopped once, at Newcastle-upon-Tyne so it was a relatively straightforward journey arriving in London (usually) at 0940 - exactly four hours later.

Jamie was in a state of excitement because business rules meant that they were able to travel First Class, something he hadn't experienced before. This merely triggered a flood of questions to Roops beforehand about whether the WiFi was better, what was the breakfast like, does the carriage have curtains, are there better toilets, do you get unlimited coffee, do you get a free newspaper, is there a dress code and Roops particular favourite question, do the seats recline?

It was little wonder that Roops had been absolutely dreading every minute of this journey. And worse, he thought, this was likely to be the first of many.

He was going to have to lay down a few ground rules early on just to ensure this relationship wasn't going to end with some form of physical injury involving a Virgin East Coast teaspoon, a laptop cable and Roops's extensive knowledge of Japanese torture techniques garnered from watching the History channel when he'd had an enforced lay off with gout.

Roops arrived at the train station at 0455 which he thought was probably ridiculously early even by his standards.

He liked to get everywhere early to give himself plenty of time to assess the surroundings, work out first if something was going to go wrong, get the best seats in the station with his back to the wall (being in a train station, he wanted to ensure everything was in front of him), get his coffee, newspapers and of course, print off his tickets.

But on this occasion, he wasn't the only one to be ridiculously early. Jamie was already there himself, waiting for Roops like an excited puppy, waving to him as he walked down the roadway into the central part of the station.

"Oh for fuck sake" thought Roops "Already. He's started already."

"How y'doing Jamie? You're up and at it early today? I hope you managed some sleep last night! Were you up trying to catch Santa out??" Roops laughed. He thought the laugh might disguise his contempt.

"Ha ha! I completely messed up my times Roops and got here way too early. I didn't want to be late, last seen chasing the train down the platform like I was in an old Ealing comedy film! I could only imagine what you'd be thinking of me if that happened!"

To be fair, Roops thought, he did have a point. And he quite liked the fact that he wanted to be early, unlike some of his other colleagues who sauntered around as if the train would wait only for them.

They picked up their tickets and headed to the train. Carriage M was the First Class section that they were in and at this time of day, was fairly quiet.

"I don't know about you," said Jamie "but I never have a clue about the seat numbering on trains. It's like they allocated them using a bingo machine, with the numbers coming out completely at random. And I was checking online - what the hell is an "airline" seat??"

Roops just smiled, thinking back to his conversation with Trevor. "I know, just don't get me started about trains. But what I do know is that the "Airline Seats" are the ones that recline ..." Roops couldn't help saying mischievously.

They sat down and started engaging in the kind of small talk that happens when two people who barely know each other end up together, when they know they've got the rest of two days stuck in each other's company.

Every topic was covered - what they did at the weekend, the restaurants they went to, the family they had to see, the football, the rugby, the darts, the snooker, the boxing, the Formula 1, the Formula 1 on Sky versus the Formula 1 on Channel 4, their favourite comedy shows, the music they like, the holidays they like going on.

It was all laid bare as they gently began to find out a bit more about each other and understood how each other thought and more importantly, operated. Roops was looking for signs that they might have some sort of common ground.

"Did this guy get it? Can I trust him? Does he know the score?" he mused "Or was he the son of Trevor, spawned by a formula from a book on infinitesimal calculus, and then neatly repackaged as a form of human being?"

He certainly seemed to be making the right noises. He liked most sports and more importantly, seemed to understand it. He drank beer with a preference for real ales and also understood enough about red wine to know the good ones from Italy, Spain and France over the weaker ones from Australia. He had a broad musical taste focusing mostly on bands that played their own instruments and wrote their own tunes and interestingly, he seemed to have a pretty obvious disregard for "the establishment". This seemed to be borne from an ongoing grudge about continuously being overlooked for all promotions and exciting project work. Roops could relate.

"So Roops, how come you agreed to go down on the train? I thought you hated the train?" asked Jamie, clearly feeling that they were getting quite close.

"Yeah, that was Trevor's idea! What he told you was what he told me as well. In his own little actuarial planet, he thought it would be good for you and I to spend time together to chat about the next couple of days. Apparently a coffee in the canteen wouldn't allow for the same experience of bonding. Still it could have been worse …"

"Could it? How??" laughed Jamie.

"The fucker could have put us on a plane to Gatwick! Thankfully I keep my views on that fairly close to my chest so he can't ever throw that one at me!" roared Roops.

"What's wrong with Gatwick then?" said Jamie, sensing a story coming on. Roops was already off and running though.

"Well, earlier you mentioned Ealing comedies. It's a similar type of thing. It's normally tricky to accurately describe flying into Gatwick particularly to someone under the age of 40, without sounding patronising, because everything about it feels as if it's something from the distant past."

"I remember growing up watching comedy programmes such as Terry & June or even George & Mildred, set in the front rooms of typical suburban households which were dressed in garish orange and brown wallpaper and furnished with lava lamps. In places, Gatwick's just like that as well - "old world modern" is how I'd describe it."

"There is some evidence that once upon a time it was trying to be up to date but judging by what I've seen, it looks like they gave up on that sometime around 1978. In other areas, in a complete contrast, it looks like how I've always imagined living in the 1960s Soviet-bloc would have been like - basically, grey and cold."

"So, in other words, it's a mass of contradictions with the occasional sign of modernity bolted onto what sat before."

Jamie sat staring at the ceiling with a quizzical look on his face, trying to work out what exactly that meant.

"It also seems to have no process to it. Invariably when you land, fate always dictates that it will be at the "wrong" terminal. Gatwick is split into two – the North terminal and the South terminal which you'd hope were named after their relative positioning between both themselves and a compass. But to assume too much in Gatwick is always a mistake – so let's just accept they are what they are and move on."

"The North terminal seems to be more the home for domestic flights with the South for International ones. I've made this assumption because when we've landed at the South terminal, we're told that we've actually landed at the International side of the airport so we need to be bussed over to the Domestic gates. That said, some domestic carriers such as EasyJet seem to be popping up in the South too so again, who's to say? Maybe they're just making it up as they go along? Perish the thought …"

Jamie leant forward smiling. He could tell this story was "long haul". He'd heard that when Roops got passionate about something he would positively purr the story. It was one of his little foibles.

"When you clamber onto the bus at the South terminal to get taken over to the North it really is a strange experience. You know what it's like when you land in Spain or Italy or basically any hot country? Getting bussed to the terminal usually means jumping on board at a remote part of the tarmac and transferred across open space to the terminal. You can see two things – vast openness with a few planes dotted around under a blue sky and then also the terminal to which you're headed."

"At Gatwick, you never see your final destination until you've reached it. You are taken through an endless number of concrete lanes and tunnels, underneath vast bleak grey buildings all of which have pipes running along the outside of them scarring like varicose veins."

"It reminds me of scenes from old 1970s US cop films like The French Connection which are really bleak and earthy. The car chases in those films and the TV shows like Kojak would invariably take you through road sections underneath browny, red metal bridges covered and surrounded by loads of pipes. This has a similar feel to it - just much slower obviously. And not as warm. And rather than being in the back of Popeye Doyle's car, you're on a battery operated bus. But otherwise, it's a perfect replication of 1970s downtown New York in one of those films!" laughed Roops.

"The pipes that run around the buildings of Gatwick are seemingly endless and filthy and it feels like there are thousands of them. You'd easily think that you'd landed at a large oil refinery by mistake. Gatwick appears to have more pipes than it needs weaving through the buildings like one huge Meccano set."

"The experience of standing on the bus, jolting left then right through these never ending concrete lanes, staring at abandoned battery powered vehicles and baggage trolleys makes you feel as if your destination is altogether something more sinister. Does life exist in this strange land? Workers are occasionally passed but they stare distant stares, faces without emotion. "

"Again, it's reminiscent of a scene from an old TV show but this time it could be an episode of Doctor Who - probably the Jon Pertwee era - about to face some strange cyborg race."

Jamie sat with his eyes wide open, listening intently.

"When the bus finally stops at an apparently random door, there's no clever swishing of electronic doors as you enter. At this terminal, they are old, heavy glass and metal doors fixed to their frames with large magnets to secure them."

"You enter the 1970s through this door. Mr Benn used to do the same thing …"

"Mr Benn?"

"Mr Benn. He wore a bowler hat and went into a dressing up shop to visit different places. Just ask your dad. It's a bit complicated. Anyway, if you're finished with the stupid questions. The flooring at Gatwick is the most hard-wearing of carpeting. Characterless, faded, tired of life, it's matched by the drudgery and blandness of the walls where they have gone to incredible lengths to make them appear the dreariest that you could possibly get. You begin to wonder whether they're protected by the National Trust as an example of "how things used to be" because surely by now, they must be deserving of even the lightest lick of paint."

"If ever an airport represented the 1970s bleakness then this is it. It's still here. It's called Gatwick."

"Have you ever been to Liverpool Jamie" Roops suddenly asked.

Jamie looked a bit startled. "Er, no …"

"Well, there's a pub there called The Grapes where The Beatles used to drink. Inside the pub, they have kept some of the original wallpaper which is framed with a glass box to help you get a feel for what the pub would have been like in those glorious days of yore and mop top haircuts. You should go. It's brilliant."

"Similarly, the bit where you first enter Gatwick as an arriving domestic passenger is one long example of what it looked like

146

when it was first built. It's designed to be the most unwelcome welcome you are ever likely to get – bar none."

"Now I appreciate that there are likely to be some far flung distant airports, possibly even former military bases which are, by someone's definition, "worse" but you'd expect them to be worse. In fact, you'd be disappointed if they weren't really dank and bleak."

"But Gatwick is meant to be a modern day airport welcoming visitors from all around the world. If this is the first experience many get of Cool Britannia, then it's completely shit."

Roops was getting louder now as he built up a rhythm, leaving Jamie to check that his fellow passengers in First Class couldn't overhear them.

"The maze of blandness that they've created seems to be designed to deliberately confuse. Occasionally, you're faced with choices – for example, steps or ramps with the assumption being that the steps should be the quicker but in an apparent riposte to logic the opposite is invariably true. Steps in this instance are no more than a diversionary tactic."

"And then there is one part of this trudge, which actually always makes me smile. Just to hamper the speed at which you might want to get to the actual exit, the Gatwick designers have very cleverly placed a series of pillars. These pillars split the corridor perfectly and beautifully to ensure that anyone walking slowly is guaranteed to hold everyone else up, creating a very long snake of increasingly disgruntled people who are unable to jump to the other "lane" by the continuation of the concrete pillars."

"Very occasionally you can see opportunities to overtake but it's only through experience that you know they're coming and you have to position yourself perfectly to take full advantage of them as they appear! You can take out 10 passengers in one go!"

"It's hilarious that in a modern day, 21st century airport, they've never actually thought about sorting this section out. It's just really, really awfully planned and thought through. I say planned, I think they've just asked their seven year old to crack on with it and see what happens."

"After this section, and more bottlenecks and escalators that don't work, you finally get to the Arrivals area which in case you're wondering Jamie, can take anything up to 25 minutes including having been on the bus from the plane, which happened just after having had two cups of coffee on a flight that lasted 90 minutes. So naturally, this means that virtually everyone who had been on the flight will now be needing to take a piss."

"And luckily for them just before leaving this area, the good people of Gatwick have installed some very modern looking toilets with, count them, not one but TWO urinals and a couple of closets should a turtle's head be poking its nose out. Cue queues."

Roops was getting more and more theatrical in his delivery of his story.

"Now - before I go on, I have to emphasise that none of this is actually the bad bit. That's still ahead of you," said Roops laughing.

"The bad bit isn't even that having landed at the South terminal, then ferried across to the North terminal, to walk through the time warp of the 1970s corridors almost wetting yourself in the process, you now have to go back to the South terminal if you want to get a train to central London. No, in a relative sense, what you've just been through should just be considered a mild irritation."

With a heightened sense of drama, Roops leant forward and lowered his voice to say "But remember Jamie, hell awaits from this point on!"

Jamie laughed out loud, loving the crassness of the story.

"When landing at any London airport, as I pointed out earlier, you become in effect just another London commuter. All the effort you've made up to that point just gets you to parity with every other London commuter in fact. And if you were ever in any doubt as to what this means, it hits you square on in the face the moment you walk into the train station at Gatwick. Because Gatwick, is by some distance, the worst airport to get into the City of London from."

"That's why when you get the PA to look at flights, it's cheaper to fly into Gatwick than the other airports. It's because if you've fallen into the trap of flying into Gatwick once, it's unlikely that you'd really want to put yourself through it again. So they try to seduce you with cheaper flight tickets ..."

"The first thing that strikes you is the long snaking queue for train tickets. What looks like hundreds of people standing in line, some business travellers but mostly holidaymakers, with bags and cases at their feet which naturally slows the movement and your progress towards actually getting your train ticket. It feels like hours just to get over that first hurdle."

"And of course, with Gatwick being an international hub, you need to throw into the mix that for many, this is their first opportunity to practice their English meaning an even longer time standing waiting on them to practice their skills in front of a ticket machine. And most of them are also a mixture of largely tired and jet-lagged holidaymakers pulling a seemingly endless supply of enormous brightly coloured suitcases behind them which they just abandon in the middle of the floor in a single moment without warning nor reason."

"And then you have the groups of usually Mediterranean youths who are notorious for just deciding to suddenly stop – in the middle of the hall and the queue - huddling around a single map, chattering furiously presumably discussing where they have actually landed."

"Up to this point, their vision of London matched the pictures on the front of their maps but so far all they've seen is concrete and pipes so they're naturally very confused. Not one sign yet of Big Ben, no Tower Bridge and definitely no red buses. Just concrete and lots of pipes."

"Abbiamo appena atterrato a New York? - ha ha! Have we just landed in New York!" I overhear them say. "Clearly the reruns of old 1970s cop shows are popular in downtown Florence!"

Jamie laughed nervously at this point "You've clearly given this a lot of thought Roops!! I think you've been struck with a bit of madness with all this travel you've been doing!"

"Yes, well that's one word that it's been described as. Anyway …"

"The problem with the design of the ticketing queue "system" is that when you finally reach the front, it's almost impossible to see where the next space at the ticket machines opens up, meaning you bear the wrath of all those behind you if you immediately fail to spot the one vacant machine. You can sense an almighty roar building behind you if you don't immediately run towards the first space."

"This then puts you under pressure to perform when you get to the machine as you feel the burning eyes of fellow passengers boring into the back of your head."

"Now, you'd think that it would be a fairly simple exercise from here to get your ticket. You'd think that and of course, you'd be completely wrong because Gatwick, and the southern parts of England, are serviced by a multiple number of rail companies and rail companies are hard-coded to only think of themselves rather than anybody who might actually want to travel on them!"

Jamie started relaxing again, laughing and smiling at Roops as the story progressed. He'd never heard anything like this!

"So when you stand, nervously, looking to identify exactly which ticket you need to get you to central London, you are faced with a paralysing amount of choice. Failure is almost guaranteed even here at Gatwick where you only have two rail companies to choose from."

"To the experienced London commuter it's easy. But they're generally really boring people who can recite their train timetable like Reginald Perrin because for four hours a day, that's all they have to do with themselves – stand on trains or on platforms staring at train timetables. Their work is merely a minor interruption to standing on a train crushed up against someone else's sternum."

"So to pair it down at Gatwick, you initially have two choices but then again it could possibly be four - it might even be more than that. I genuinely don't really know because I shut my eyes and just press the button that says London Bridge!" laughed Roops.

"I don't really know if I'm travelling at Peak Time. It should be Peak Time but it's taken me so bloody long just to get here that it could now be mid-morning and now Off-Peak (and by the way, "Off-Peak" seems to get hyphenated even although "Peak Time" isn't - I hate this abuse of the English language!)."

"The choices I think you have are whether you want to go to London Victoria which they say is on the Gatwick Express or whether you want to go to London Bridge."

"London Victoria is in the west end, near Buckingham Palace although when you reach there and walk out into the street, you couldn't feel further from the most recognisable view in the United Kingdom. Instead, you're faced with row upon row of cheap discount shops, Bureaux de Change and dodgy looking steak houses."

"However, we don't want to go the west end, we want to go to the City and that's not served well by Gatwick."

"If you want to go to the City, you need to head to London Bridge rail station meaning your choices appear to be either Southern Rail or ThamesLink. But then again, ThamesLink seems to want to take you to somewhere else. I literally have no idea if both go to London Bridge, or if it's only one because nobody tells you."

"Also, once you've bought your ticket and try look for which platform, and then train, you need to get to take you to London Bridge, you're faced with more confusion."

"You see, it's almost impossible to determine quickly where you should be because London Bridge is merely a stop on the route. It's not the final stop so the board doesn't scream "London Bridge" – you have to look at every train on the Departure's Board and wait for it to tell you which station each train stops at scrolling through the screen. This takes ages because they're more interested in telling you if the train has a trolley service and toilet rather than helping you to your platform at the right time."

"It's just so fucking shit, Jamie. It really is!" Roops was getting more animated now.

"The confusion doesn't stop here because when you get onto the platform, every train that arrives seems to go to London and even London Bridge – but the attendant, who has finally shown their face, will tell you that you don't have the right ticket for that train provider or alternatively they'll suggest that you don't get that train to London Bridge. Instead go to East Croydon - or is it South Croydon - and change there to get a quicker train to London Bridge …"

"Thankfully, the only respite you get is that Southern Rail is one of the worst rail companies in Britain and when it's not on strike, it's broken down or perhaps even just having a bad day and has decided to stay in bed. This therefore reduces the choices in front of you by roughly one half."

Jamie was delighted with this story so far - this could be the most entertaining two days of his life he thought!!

Roops continued on his rant. Jamie spotted that when he started a sentence with "To be fair …" it usually meant he was about to be really unfair …

"To be fair, none of this is actually the fault of Gatwick airport other than it's located in a really crap part of the country, serviced by one of the most crap train operators on a railway network which is so confusing that your brain explodes just trying to work it all out."

"And that means that it's the worst possible airport to fly into when you want a quick and easy start to your day if that's meant to be in London city centre."

"Phew! So don't go to Gatwick then?" said Jamie, hoping that he could draw this very entertaining but very long story to a close.

"Correct Jamie, don't go to Gatwick because more than any other airport, when you land there you genuinely become more of a London commuter than you would be at any other of the airports."

"You see, the trains going into London Bridge don't start at Gatwick – they've already been trundling along the English countryside from Brighton (it seems), happily picking up more and more weary looking passengers with their little foldaway Brompton bikes to the point that the train cannot hold a single additional person – which is a piffling point really because they will do everything within their power to actually get that additional person on board to make the experience for them and everyone else as utterly miserable as possible."

"I stand on that train bewildered by the contradiction of it all. Most people on this train are travelling into the City of London which is one of the world's main economic centres. This is a main artery of the lifeblood to the world economy, powering the United Kingdom's place at the top table of places to invest in. And yet the people who are powering this are currently crammed tight, nose to nose on a train which could break at any moment, breathing in everyone else's air, rubbing against people in the most unhygienic way possible."

"Christ" thought Jamie, "he's really not finished …"

"This isn't the modern world – it's the Third World in suits. It's degrading, filthy and cynical towards people who have no choice other than to use this as their primary mode of transport to get to their work."

"So if I was asked for one piece of advice, and I bear Gatwick no ill will, it would be that if you're travelling into the City you should avoid flying into Gatwick airport at all costs."

"Do not be seduced by the cheaper air tickets on offer – it's a complete and utter, absolute false economy."

"It's the closest thing to a guarantee that wherever you are going, you will be late. You will be tired, you will be sweaty, you will be in a horrendous mood all day, you will question your own sanity and you will very possibly catch some nasty illness."

"Finished now?"

"Yes. Well almost … You see, you will almost certainly want to talk about your experience to every single person you come into contact with that day which means you will effectively become just like every other person that works in the City of London. You will become "one of them". You will have that badge of honour where your only topic of social conversation is your horrendous journey into work. That's all that the people who work in London ever talk about."

"People who once upon a time had personalities are now really, really boring because their trains keep breaking."

"Brilliant" said Jamie "Absolutely brilliant! How do you cope with all of this?"

"Well, not easily. I'll let you into a wee secret. For years, all of this would really get to me. It still does to some extent but I'm trying to learn to control it. I'm not sure I'll ever be "cured" if there's actually anything to cure as such. But I write fictitious emails to anyone who really annoys me. It's a form of catharsis. I never actually send them, I just write them. It lets me vent without offending anyone anymore."

"You mean you used to send them?" a startled Jamie asked.

"Sometimes I did, not these ones but I got so frustrated I would send nasty unrelated notes and I was just an arse. Now I write these notes to sort of cleanse me of the experience. I keep them in my Notes pages on my iPhone and sometimes read them back over. I find I learn quite a lot about myself."

"Oh" said Jamie, not really knowing where to look. This was Roops talking. And he was exposing a vulnerability.

"I even wrote a Gatwick airport email! Do you want to see it? I'm actually quite proud of it - I think it's quite clever!"

"Too right I do!" said Jamie excitedly.

Roops pulled out his phone and opened up the email taking a quick glance at it, smiling as he handed it over.

Jamie settled back and started reading.

"Dear Sir or Madam,

I am writing to congratulate you.

In the UK today, we're living through a period where it is fashionable for all things to be "retro", harking back to a time when things were just much simpler. I'm talking about a time when mobile phones didn't exist, Spangles were the sweet of choice, the halfpenny was still in circulation and the nation came to a standstill every time The Osmonds appeared on Top of The Pops.

Retro fashion is making a big return with new editions of the parka and the Harrington jacket, Doc Marten's boots and the peaky blinder cap. Retro pubs are making a comeback too, filling themselves with a wide range of craft beers served in old metal tankards in front of roaring fires. And then there's my own personal favourite, retro music with the return of the vinyl record.

So you can imagine my complete surprise and delight when landing at Gatwick recently to see that you have sternly resisted all attempts to modernise and delivered what must be the UK's, if not the world's, first and only "retro airport".

It's an absolutely genius move – "visionary" doesn't even begin to describe it.

From the lack of aesthetics to the broken escalators, the attempts at hampering passenger progress collecting their bags to the sparse locations of public conveniences, and of course the overcrowded train station with staff numbers so scarce that you'd think we were in the middle of the 1970s three-day week - you have gone that extra mile to deliver an experience that I previously only learned about from the ramblings of my geriatric and senile grandparents.

Your "piece de resistance" is of course the blue signage which boldly proclaims Gatwick airport at every opportunity – it screams "Abigail's Party". If only you were able to put it against orange and brown patterned wallpaper with a lava lamp alongside you'd complete the look – but I suppose you don't want to look too ridiculous. Just a little bit ridiculous seems to be enough.

Yours faithfully

Rupert X Wardhaugh"

Jamie sat laughing out loud. He wasn't quite sure what he'd read but he enjoyed it. But more importantly, he felt touched that Roops was so willing to open up to him like this. He neither expected this level of engagement nor had he ever suspected these vulnerabilities in Roops. It made him think and reflect.

Chapter 14
When I Live My Dream

"So Jamie, who's this new company that Trevor wants you to start working with? What do you know about them?" asked Roops.

"If I'm honest, not a huge amount. I've checked them out on the internet and they seem to be a fairly new start-up with a couple of people having split off from a bigger group. I think you might know some of them …? The person we've been lined up to see though is a new girl called Jess Montgomery. I've checked her out on LinkedIn and she's very new, straight out of university and has started in their Marketing department."

"Do we know what they want from us yet?" asked Roops "Or do I suspect that they're about to tell us their plans for world domination within two years and that they'll differentiate themselves from everyone else by being different (whilst of course, not being different at all …!)".

Jamie detected a world weariness in Roops.

"Who knows" said Jamie. "I think there's an element of them needing to get to know us because they're new and we have a certain position in the market. If they don't engage with us, they'll never really get a feel for how they penetrate it"

"And Jess" asked Roops. "She's new? Straight out of university?"

"Yes, I think so." offered Jamie.

"Magic. So we're dealing with a dreamer then. My second one today."

Jess Montgomery was like any other 23 year old who had just completed her university degree in Marketing and Hospitality.

Almost leaping off the silver screen from the film Jerry Maguire, she was ready to take on the world, make her mark and earn her fortune. Her dreams were endless matched only by her bountiful supplies of ambition and energy.

She grew up in a little town in the middle of nowhere, where it was idyllic in so many ways with lambs gambolling across open glades, the birds always in full song and the local hunt riding furiously as their hounds caught yet another poor, unsuspecting fox ready to tear its near lifeless body piece by piece, humanely of course.

"This is just perfect" she thought, as she laid back in her garden deck chair, sipping another long Pimms, the ice gently chinking on the side of the glass whilst the mint rather unglamorously stuck to her front tooth. Nobody was around to point out this potential embarrassment but anyway, who's to care?

It always seemed to be sunny there, in this little piece of heaven.

Jess closed her eyes and dreamt. Dreamt of corporate stardom, of being front-page news and the cover star of national magazines. Dreamt of leading huge teams all who looked up to her and waited with bated breath on her every word. She was a visionary and a pioneer. She could see so many things that were wrong with the world just waiting for her to grab it by the scruff of the neck and change it. But she'd never do it here.

She had to move to "The Best City In The World".

This both excited Jess and scared her. She had never been to the large Metropolis before, only read about it and seen it on TV. She could imagine herself living there but only through the lens of the camera she'd already seen it through.

Her own town was like any other small town. It didn't offend anyone and was perfectly reasonable to live in. Like many other towns, it had its own railway station, a town centre with an M&S, Starbucks, Costa, Pret a Manger and of course, a Dorothy Perkins to dress the discerning churchgoers.

Its pubs were in plentiful supply and everyone was really friendly, always offering you the time of day, a helping hand when needed and a plethora of Conservative Party brochures to keep you on the straight and narrow.

There was a great little local bus service which was like something from All Creatures Great and Small or even Postman Pat. The driver was known to everyone, always very friendly, happy to stop in between appointed Bus Stops and even helped old ladies on and off with their heavy shopping bags. This town had manners aplenty.

To the young 23 year old, this was the sort of sleepy town that she wanted, no needed, to escape from.

"How could a place like this ever accommodate a future titan of industry?" she would think to herself as she picked more lavender and rosemary from her mother's garden. "I have to make the leap. I have to move to The Best City In The World."

Jess broke the news to her mother and father, Barbara and Giles, who accepted this stoically. They privately feared for their daughter but with typical British spirit, refused to even discuss this with each other let alone Jess herself.

"Off you go then darling. Good luck and please write" her father said in muffled tones as he sucked on his pipe.

"Dad, remember, I showed you how to text. If you go to the end of the garden, you get a decent signal from there. We never need to be out of touch," she said, slightly exasperated at silly old dad. He was a bit of a twat but she loved him.

Jess packed several suitcases and waved goodbye to her parents who stood at the front gate to watch their daughter head off into the sunset. She strode purposefully into the ticket office of the local railway station with no time to waste. The next train to The Best City In The World was due to leave in 15 minutes and if she was to get her lucky seat, she needed to be ready.

"Hello Bertie" she said to the ticket master, "I'm off to The Best City In The World – could I get a SINGLE ticket please?"

"A SINGLE Jess? You better be watching yourself with those fancy ideas of yours! There's no good to be had in those parts, you mark my words. Anyway, that'll be £54.10."

"My God Bertie, I'm not building the High Speed Rail Link you know! I only want to get the train down the road …!!" she laughed, as she handed over her father's emergency Coutts bank card.

"This is SO exciting. I must get some sandwiches and those foam banana things for the train. "

"You take care my love and remember, they still speak the same language as us. It just sounds like they're trying not to …" Bertie roared with laughter. He did like his own jokes.

It was a Sunday and Jess's journey to The Best City In The World was uneventful. Quiet even. In just over two hours, she arrived at her final destination.

"This is it" she thought, "this is the future – my future."

Jess had rented a small bedsit roughly 12 miles from the centre of The Best City In The World. She had expected better things from her first flat, maybe a view of the river or even across the skyline of the City itself. But this would have to do for now.

"This keeps me real" she thought "And it will sound better in my autobiography if I started off somewhere like this. Humble beginnings and all that."

The bedsit was situated in a block with 5 others, fronted in bland brick with peeling paint around the condensation covered windows. Inside had a small functional kitchen which had tiles badly in need of some new grout.

Her settee doubled up as her bed and had clearly seen some "action" given the tremendous sag in the centre. These were springs that had had their bounce well and truly bounced.

The bathroom housed a small electric boiler and a bath with shower curtain around it. The shower head drooped until water came through it when it raised its head slightly in mock deference to the proposed recipient of its gentle dribble.

"Character building" thought Jess as she settled down for her first night. Big day tomorrow after all – day one of the rest of her life!

Jess was up at the crack of dawn – 7.15am – ready to take on the world. After a gentle breakfast of toast spread lightly with marmalade, a pot of her favourite tea and some Alpen listening to

Radio 2, she laid out her wardrobe to consider her attire for the day.

"Dress for the job above you" she thought. "Now where's my power blouse, power dress and power heels?" as she set the ironing board up to sharpen the seams.

"This is going to be just perfect. Me and The Best City In The World are made for each other!"

At 8.30, Jess tottered down the street to find her nearest mode of transport. She was starting at 9am and couldn't wait to experience the full delights of The Best City In The World and its amazing transport infrastructure.

In the distance, she could see a familiar sign which she recognised as the railway station. "That'll do me nicely" she thought.

Jess approached the ticket office, which appeared to be closed. "This is strange" she thought. "Bertie was always open on weekdays and this is early morning? There's maybe somewhere else I need to go"

She searched and searched the platform looking for another ticket office but all she could see were closed, locked doors with absolutely no information. Then at the end of the platform she saw a man in a bright tabard, emblazoned with a railway company logo and the words "Here to help you" underneath. Her veritable knight in hi-vis armour.

"Oh excuse me sir – I'm new to this part of The Best City In The World and I need to get to the City for the first day of my new job" she panted.

The man looked at her and said "You're in the wrong place love" and he walked away from her.

Jess was astonished. Who was this blaggard, this imposter? She chased after him.

"Excuse me, excuse me – I just need a ticket to the City. I just need to get from A to B …" she cried, exasperated.

The man roared with laughter!

"You've just asked for the impossible lady! Everybody just wants to get from A to B in this City – and it's the hardest thing in the world to do!"

"All our trains are knackered today anyway. The guards have gone on strike because the train company have said the drivers can control the doors themselves"

"And can they?" asked Jess.

"Of course they can, darling – but that's not the point. If the drivers controlled the doors, there'd be no guards – and no guards, means no more strikes and where would that leave us? It would be bleeding anarchy!"

Jess stood for a moment, trying to work out if that did indeed describe anarchy or if this guy was just taking the piss.

"Anyway, you want to try the Tube. It's that way," he said pointing to a tunnel at the bottom of some stairs.

"Well thank you sir" she muttered to herself, turning away.

Jess headed towards the Tube station trying to digest the recent counsel regarding Trade Union relations. It was certainly a different viewpoint to the leaflets her father used to bring home from his Club she thought. She remembered they said Workers' Rights were not to be encouraged because otherwise before we knew it we'd be living like the French.

The Tube station was an amazing sight to behold. It seemed to be an old Victorian building with ornate tiling around the roof, below which were hundreds of people moving en-masse, very slowly, slightly jostling, looking mightily impatient as they approached the mechanical barrier system.

"This looks fun" she thought "I'll be just like a businessman on the news". In the distance she could hear a low rumbling noise. "Well at least the trains are running here" she thought, relieved.

She headed into the throng and very quickly became mightily unsteady. Despite her best attempts, she couldn't move in the direction she wanted to. Nobody would acknowledge her existence or make eye contact with her. Nobody made eye contact with anyone in fact. Personal space was an alien concept here. They were just all so rude! What at first looked like gentle jostling was now like being in the middle of a rugby scrum.

"Even The Fox and Hound back home on New Year's Eve is easier to contend with!" she thought.

Finally, Jess reached the ticket barrier which she saw was marked "Contactless".

"Right," she thought "almost there". She stepped towards the grey gates which slammed right into her body, trapping the briefcase she held in front of her.

"They're Contactless gates luv, get a move on!" said an impatient voice from behind her.

She turned and wailed "I'm trying to be Contactless with them! Can't you see that? This bloody gate just about cut me in two! I didn't want to touch it!!"

"You didn't touch your card on the reader you dozy mare!" said the irritated voice.

"What do you mean I didn't touch it? It says Contactless! I'm not meant to touch it!" she shrilled "How can I touch something when it's meant to be Contactless? That doesn't make bloody sense!"

"C'mon luv, stop pissing around. We all need to get to work. You've either got card clash, and confused the hell out of the thing, or no money at all. Either way, I don't give a damn. Move out of the way and go to the ticket office."

Jess retreated in defeat, furious. What was that he said about "clack cosh"? Or was it "hard slash"?? What was it he said? She'd never heard an insult like it before. Bertie was right – they were trying to talk a different language.

She saw the ticket booth over to her right and forcing her way through the tidal wave of bodies going in the opposite direction at last made it through.

The ticket office was actually no more than a small plastic window cut into the wall with a big woman sitting behind the counter. She didn't even need to raise her head to see who was in front of her to begin speaking.

"Yes" said an electronic voice.

"Ha ha. She sounds like Cher on Believe!" thought Jess. "How cute!"

"Erm, I'm sorry madam but I'm confused. I need to get to the City really quickly and I tried to use your Tube but the gates wouldn't open. Apparently I might have caused Dick Dosh? Try as I might, I promise you I didn't touch them just like the "Contactless" sign told me but they still wouldn't open. I mustn't be looking at them in the right way. Anyway, could you help me?"

"What line you want?" huffed the voice, still completely disinterested and still not even raising her head.

"Line? What do you mean Line?? I want to get a Tube? Nobody told me about a Line?! This place is ridiculous! All I want is to get from A to B? Why is that so bloody difficult???"

The ticket woman looked up and roared with laughter!

"A to B?? Lady – we have possibly the worst and most confusing travel infrastructure in the world. We have trains designed in the 1940s when gentlemen in bowler hats and brollies would saunter to the Bank. We have severe overcrowding and the trains have air conditioning (an open window at the end of each carriage) designed for half the amount of people on board. Getting a Tube to the City at this time will involve at least three changes for you. At each point, you will leave one overcrowded train to shuffle towards a different platform even more crowded than the one before. When you finally reach your destination – in about an hour and a half – you'll be so sodden with sweat that people will think you'd swam there."

"An hour and a half!!" cried Jess. "I can't wait an hour and a half! I need to be there in 20 minutes! There must be a quicker way??"

"Have you thought of getting a taxi?" chuckled the woman. "They'll offer you some travel advice".

Jess picked up her things and stormed back out into the sunlight above, increasingly furious. "This must be The Best City In The World - every man and his dog wants to get in this morning" she mused sarcastically.

Wandering down the road in search of a cab, she noticed how cold and lifeless everybody was. Nobody looked anyone in the eye let alone nodding any gentle morning felicitations – nobody seemed to acknowledge the existence of any other human being in fact. Everyone just got on with their job of getting to where they needed to be but with what seemed to be an underlying, simmering fury.

About thirty metres away, Jess spotted an old black taxi spewing out its diesel across the street. Its yellow light above the front window was on – she knew this was a good thing and instantly thrust her hand out to grab the driver's attention.

"Can you take me to the City please? And I need you to be quick …" said Jess

"You'll be bleeding lucky!" snorted the taxi driver.

"Oh for fuck sake! What is it with this place?" screamed an exasperated Jess, "I JUST WANT TO GET FROM A TO B!!"

The taxi driver roared with laughter!

"Why is that such a ridiculous question sir? Every person I've said it to has just laughed in my face?"

"Let me tell you sweetheart" said the driver, in a scene straight out of a 1970s TV show, "this might label itself as The Best City In The World but frankly that doesn't mean one jot if you live here. Sure, if you're a tourist and you want to see the bright lights, the latest shows, see movie stars attend premieres, eat at top restaurants and stay in massively over-priced hotels then this place has more to offer than any city in the world. But let's be honest, that's not how you'd define "The Best" – or you shouldn't anyway."

"Our City could be The Greatest City Ever or whatever they want to market it as. But until they start showing the people who live and work here a bit of respect then it's lost."

"All you can do in the meantime is accept it's shit. You'll have a life of paying over the odds, getting screwed by the system, being barged into by people, barging into people yourself, smelling other people's smells, getting smelly yourself, getting interrupted and distracted, being held to mercy by a public transport structure which is being managed by people who haven't the faintest idea what they're doing, who in turn are at the mercy of the unions who completely understand what they're doing. They want to make your already miserable life even more miserable – because they're jealous that you work in an industry that doesn't need to rely on their tactics just to get a morsel of what they want. Yes, they'll call it Workers' Rights and all that – but Workers' Rights are already enshrined in the law. They're doing it out of spite. Why else would they bring 300,000 people to a standstill just because … Well, know what I mean?"

"And then there's the Mayor – he's useless. What we need is somebody who can run things, not an elected politician who's only in it for his own vicarious needs. When everything around him is falling apart – the Tube, the trains, the roads what does he do? He causes more disruption by introducing a bleeding bike lane! I mean, a bike lane!! Keeps them out the way I suppose but it's causing more delays than good now. Know what I mean?"

"At least I have my Arsenal to keep me going. But bleeding Wenger's stayed way too long – he hasn't won anything in years. Keeps tinkering and letting The Chelsea get ahead. He was great once but that was all down to Tony Adams – god bless him – and King Thierry Henry. Gawd, he was something else – could hit a sixpence from thirty yards that one. He was special. And now he's on Sky Sports with that bleeding Gary Neville. He never knows when to shut up – always got something to say about everything him. I hated him as a player and hate him even more now."

"Just like Fergie – all those Jocks have got far too much to say for themselves. Independence? INDE-BLOODY-PENDENCE?? They should let us all vote for that one – I'd give them independence in a minute and let them drown in their own oil. No one else would have anything useful to do with it – it's worthless now. So they can just fuck off and take bloody Uber off our hands whilst they're at it!"

Jess's head was spinning. She had absolutely no idea what this man was on about. He'd just leapt from calling her sweetheart to proposing the division of the Union in around two minutes flat … And all she'd asked was why getting from A to B was such an amusing question to everyone who heard it.

"Sorry to interrupt sir – but how close are we? It's my first day at work and already I'm really late …?"

"It's the roads love! This bleeding new Mayor has decided to dig them all up! Can't get moving for love nor money. Everywhere we turn there's more diggers than a JCB convention. I know a lane though. We'll be there in 5 minutes."

Jess was bewildered and haunted. This was the worst journey she had ever, ever endured – and she'd been to Norfolk where the staple mode of transport was usually fuelled by straw.

What was this strange place she'd entered into? She fell into a deep dreamy daze.

Finally, finally … she made it to her new work. A little sanctuary of potential peace and tranquillity where she could hide in perfect isolation.

"Jess! You've arrived! We were worried about you! How was your journey?" asked her new boss, Penny.

Jess took a deep breath but couldn't speak. She just stared ahead vacantly, unable to communicate, unable to make eye contact. Whatever last bits of resistance she'd had were wiped clean from her in the final minutes of the tortuous taxi fare.

"Don't worry about it" Penny said "you can tell me about it later. Let's get you a nice cup of tea. Our guests have arrived."

Jess looked at her in horror. She could barely breathe, let alone see anyone. She didn't even know where the loos were and already, she was being asked to meet people! After the journey she'd just had, she hated people - she had no need to be seeing more now!

"Come on" Penny said in a smooth and reassuring voice "I'm coming with you. Just sit and watch for now. I've known one of the guys for years - he's a pussycat. He doesn't know I'm with this firm now so it'll be a nice surprise for us all!"

"Hello Roops, I heard you were coming along today so I thought I'd join you!"

"Ha ha! Penny!! What are you doing here?? I never knew you had moved?"

"Yeah, well, you know what it's like. I needed a bit of a change and this opportunity with Tom came along. It gives me the chance to get away from the bureaucracy and red tape of the old place. I reckon I'll actually be able to get things done. Talking of which, this is Jess Montgomery. I managed to recruit her in around about six weeks - the old place would have put her through eight interviews over four months … Be nice though, it's her very first day with us!"

Roops, completely forgetting that Jamie was to take the lead was in full charm offensive. "Hello Jess, I'm Rupert Wardhaugh - it's a pleasure to meet you."

"And I'm Jamie Sylvester" butted in Jamie throwing a sharp glance to Roops. "I'm going to be your point of contact gong forward".

"Pleased to meet you both Jamie and Rupert …" replied Jess.

"No, call him Roops, Jess" said Penny and Jamie simultaneously.

"Nobody will know who you're talking about if you say Rupert - we'll all be looking around the room for a crusty old army major or something!" added Roops himself.

"Uh, ok" said Jess. "I must apologise for how I look. I've had the most horrendous journey into the office today. It seems that everything is stuck or on strike and apparently, according to my taxi driver, Arsene Wenger isn't doing too well either …"

"Oh don't start me on strikes" said Roops. "I once wrote to the Head of the Unions about that …"

"Oh jeez!" said Penny "what are you like … c'mon, let's you and I go and grab a coffee and we can let these two get to know each other. What's the worst that can happen?"

"So you still writing those ridiculous emails Roops?" Penny laughed as they settled down in the large whitewashed meeting area of her new office.

"Ha ha! Yeah, well you know what I was like." said Roops sheepishly. "They keep me amused and they're completely harmless. Do you want to see my one to the unions? It'll be hard to disagree with any point I make!"

"Go on then. But you're forgetting that I was Chairperson of the Students Union at uni Roops … deep down, I'm a red under the bed!" Penny shrilled.

"Right, read this and I'll grab the coffees."

Roops's email to the train and tube workers unions:

"Dear Sir or Madam or "Brothers",

Whilst I appreciate that we live in a democracy, and part of the freedom that this gives means that your right to strike is embedded within Workers' Rights, I can't help thinking that recently, you've sort of lost sight of the point a bit?

You see, in the good old days, when workers went on strike, it was to cause maximum inconvenience and cost to those who you had fallen out with. This was mostly your employer or as you might refer to them, the fat capitalist pigs.

174

That was fair enough - in some sense, it was good to see people standing up for themselves. The general public would carry some sympathy with you and with our Great British sense of fair play, we probably all wanted to see you, the poor downtrodden little guy, win.

The public, in a show of support would simply switch to a different provider whilst the strike went on meaning they weren't too inconvenienced by your selfish actions.

And this is the point that you're missing. When you go on strike and turn London into one big traffic jam, everybody suffers. Absolutely bleeding everybody but most of all, it's potentially the very people who would normally like to support you, who suffer most.

Let's be honest, most people are fundamentally selfish and what you do impacts everybody in London. And now they hate you for it.

As far as I was aware, you're not at war with me? I haven't done anything to hamper your right to work? I'm not the one who has proposed a change to your working conditions?

But you've turned me against you - I now basically hate you for making me walk all day in the pouring rain, making me late for meetings or having to completely change my whole schedule - just so that you can take a day off.

Don't patronise me that you're fighting for my safety. You're not - I can look after myself thank you. All over the world I get off and on trains with no guards and some with no drivers - the DLR is a prime example - and I seem to be doing OK. These trains even seem to run more to time without your intervention!

And how has it all worked out for you? Because whilst you were sitting at home watching Channel 4 Racing or down the pub with your Socialist Worker pals, the London economy was suffering.

Well done - great job.

And so next time you complain that a passenger speaks to you in a rude tone or maybe scowls at you or even shouts at you in desperation when you're being a complete jobsworth (get the irony there!!), just remember that you have done absolutely nothing to deserve their loyalty or respect.

Absolutely nothing.

Yours
Rupert X Wardhaugh"

Chapter 15
The Loneliest Guy

Roops and Jamie headed off to their hotel at around 1730 after a long day of various meetings. For Jamie, it had been an eye-opener and not quite the glamour he'd thought it was going to be.

He was initially quite pleased that Roops had entrusted him to the first meeting with Jess on his own, until that is that Roops confessed he couldn't really be bothered with her and fancied catching up with Penny instead.

"So actually what you're saying is that I was completely undermined ..." thought Jamie. "Whatever ..."

Jamie was at least pleased that he'd managed to see a bit of London from a different perspective for the first time but in the end, he couldn't really care about that. He was knackered from the travelling to and the subsequent travelling between meetings, and also from just concentrating on what was going on around him.

Whilst not all plain sailing, he'd learned a lot from Roops in such a short space of time already. His knowledge seemed to be encyclopaedic. He had so much experience and to some extent, it left Jamie a bit demoralised.

But for now, they were heading to the hotel.

Roops had explained to Jamie that for any regular business traveller, it made absolutely no sense to endure what is potentially five or more hours of travelling, followed by seven hours of work to then do it all again in reverse within the same day. It made much more sense to maximise your time, stay overnight or perhaps even, two. That way, you're not constrained by time at the end of the first day and can have a more genteel start to the following one or even squeeze in a little extra meeting in a very civilised fashion over breakfast.

And of course, because you're likely to stay somewhere fairly central, you won't need to endure the commute the following morning. So for once, you win and are actually ahead of the game with those around you. Jamie loved the thought of this. Being in the centre of London without having to travel there. Genius.

Roops started to explain all the potential outcomes of the night ahead.

"Staying down in London means you could spend the evening working a little later in the office, catching up on some work, doing extra emails, planning for the following day and getting some valuable thinking time without the distractions of your usual office," he started.

"Then, you can take a gentle saunter to your hotel, taking in the delights of the City skyline and watch the poor locals prepare for the battle of the evening commute ahead."

"You can then enjoy some time alone to do what you want to do. Take a stroll along the riverbank, go to a museum or exhibition, maybe take in the theatre or head to the cinema. If you're feeling particularly energetic, you might decide to go to the gym or head outside for a run."

"After that you eat, and because you're in London there is every type of restaurant on every corner – it has an Aladdin's cave of world cuisine to tempt you and your personal weaknesses. You can journey around every corner of the world in one small bite."

"Later, after wandering aimlessly back to your hotel, you might run a bath in the gloriously large tub, garnished with the luxury oils which come in an array of exotic flavours such as Blossoming Honeysuckle, Black Pepper or even Tobacco Oud. Face towels cleverly made to look like small dogs will be placed beside the bath."

"The bath towels will be soft to the skin but just crisp enough to dry you completely, smelling like they'd been rolled in fresh rose petals."

"Your bed will be huge and inviting. On it will be six big, white, fluffy, plumped up pillows so large that you'd think you were sleeping on the clouds of Zeus himself. They'll smell of fresh meadows on a warm summer's day and as you rest your weary head on them, you'll be taken off to lands where only you know."

"If the evening was a jazz album, it would have been a Miles Davis album. If it was a symphony, it would have been written by Beethoven. If the night touched perfection, you'd probably call it Blackstar."

Of course, when Roops described it like this, it made Jamie highly suspicious. Roops was never that positive about anything. Jamie smelled a rat.

"C'mon Roops - I'm not buying any of this shit. What's it really like?" probed Jamie.

The sort of idyll that Roops was describing and the idyll that the hotels want to portray is probably only available to the privileged few, the people staying in the The Savoy or The Dorchester and those in London for a recreational visit.

"Well, for the occasional traveller, the hotels describe themselves this way to present a world with no irritations and upsets and where, for those looking for the extra special bit of "me time" now and again, can disappear in their own little haven for a short time without anybody to disrupt them. These people even ask for a pillow menu!"

"Most business travellers however are working to a budget and are therefore lured by the hotels that don't make them feel as cheap as they actually are. Nobody likes to accept that they are actually working to within a budget after all."

"The whole image of the businessman, with his £300 brogues, buffed leather briefcase, Tumi travel case and cashmere overcoat, portrays an image of wealth and haughty success. It's an image that contradicts the indignity of having to stand in line, waiting to check into a Travelodge or Best Western. So the hotels play to this ego and dish out comforting words which say "we're not as crap as we used to be"."

"The hotel industry now recognises that business travellers have had it pretty rough for years and have started getting their act together for which credit has to be offered to them (although there is a strong suspicion that increased competition is really behind their motivation to clean themselves up)."

"It wasn't that far back that a business hotel – which basically means one that charges roughly £150 per night in keeping with standard budgetary limits – was a very poor and often filthy experience."

That evening, Roops and Jamie met up for some dinner, or more accurately two pizzas and a couple of beers which was about the only thing they could buy within their budget.

Using his best "old sea dog" impersonation, Roops began another lengthy monologue to the poor suffering Jamie, on the perils of business travel. Jamie just smiled in resignation of his fate.

"In those days, the rooms were basically glued together with some old wood and brown vinyl stuff. You were always scared to lay your case down on top of them in case the whole thing collapsed. The décor was beyond bland to the point that they made Gatwick look like a kaleidoscope of colour, and in those days, the rooms were invariably used by both smokers and non-smokers so they stank like a working men's club from the 1950s."

"The doors were horrendous and shook and bent when you opened them. Sometimes, they had bits falling off them or holes in the panelling. And of course, they would have had really dodgy locks that made strange noises when they engaged and they all had keys to get in, not credit card things."

"The furniture in the room used the same plywood and brown vinyl combination but with the desk area having added staining from the teacups supplied with the "Teasmaid" which was a prehistoric machine that made hot drinks. The wood would be chipped and the chair would carry its own "special staining" on its rough fabric seat."

"The toilet and baths were made from traditional porcelain however it seemed that they were only properly functional if left with a veneer of dirt on them with the toilet in particular seeming never to require any cleaning fluid - ever. It represented a far more accurate history of every visitor to the room than any reception guest book ever could."

"It was also important that a considerable amount of hair was left in the plug holes and what remained had to go on the floor. There was nothing quite like the feeling of entering the bathroom to

181

have the hair of a previous guest weave and tangle between your toes. It gave you a warm glow to know that you were never really alone …"

Jamie winced at this point as he bit into his pizza, the legs of melted mozzarella dripping down his face like strands of hair on a carpet.

"Beds of course had to be lumpy and they used blankets and sheets rather than duvets to provide the maximum possibility of an allergic reaction. The maid would make up the bed in a way that meant these sheets were so impossibly tight against the mattress that you most likely needed Vaseline to help you to actually get under the covers! And if you weren't careful, any rags or nicks on your toenails would catch on the way in meaning you would scream in pain as they tugged against the fabric of the sheet."

"The windows in the room had gaps around their frames meaning complete exposure to the external elements all throughout the night. Cold winds in the winter, unbearable heat and a sizeable dose of pollen in the summer."

"And then there was the television. These were generally like the one that your granddad watched the 1966 World Cup Final on, probably made by Bush or Rediffusion or some other long lost company. These old things needed a few minutes to warm up when you switched them on and there was no chance of them ever being stolen given they weighed roughly the same as a small car!"

Jamie laughed at this "Was that ever a possibility??"

"But it was the choice of viewing that lives long on the memory," Roops announced in a tone that suggested he was getting to the good part of his story.

"Over and above the usual terrestrial channels, they also offered "special" viewing options for the lonely traveller."

"Lovingly known as "Tug TV", these channels offered the viewer the chance to both learn a new language, mostly Swedish, and also have a remarkable insight into the daily habits of European housewives who all seemed to be going through a terrible run of form with their washing machines or general plumbing!"

Roops roared with laughter at this point as he fondly remembered the general gist of the stories involved.

"Thankfully a heavily moustachioed hero of the hour would arrive just in time to give the lady's pipes a proper cleaning, with her in return giving his Dime bar a very good polishing by way of thanks - it would appear to taste much better when it was clean!" Roops roared!

"But as all of this was on an old-style-Pay-Per-View basis they had this thing call a "2 minute preview" window, which basically meant you could watch for two minutes before deciding whether or not you wanted to shell out £5.99 for the whole film."

"If you did opt to watch the whole thing, or just weren't quick enough, you would end up with an ominous "Room Service 2" entry on your hotel bill the following morning. The embarrassment of paying for that, especially as there was no Express Check Out on those days, in front of the young lady on reception was the ultimate "Walk of Shame". Mind you, she was usually more embarrassed than you because she could see exactly what you'd been watching!!"

Roops snorted as he told the story to Jamie. "And you thought we were all off on a jolly for all these years!!"

"The world's changed now though," he said, thinking he could hear his grandfather saying exactly the same thing forty years earlier. "These modern hotels are straight out of Ikea catalogues, all pristine, sleek, efficient beasts. They're brightly lit, clean and highly polished with sharp lines everywhere."

"The rooms can be initially appealing with their mostly white plastic furniture straight out of one of these "modern design" magazines that they handily leave on the coffee table. But in the end, they're just rooms like any other room. And by the way, why do hotels think that most of their guests have any sort of interest at all in furniture design?"

"The biggest difference now of course is that most hotels will have industrial strength WiFi to allow for all sorts of viewing activity to be done via mobile phones and tablets. So it's not just Swedish that you get to learn!"

"Once, such were the similarities between your hotel room and a German Prisoner of War camp, you'd be forgiven for thinking that the metronomic thumping coming from the adjacent room was Steve McQueen throwing his baseball against the wall. These days it's merely some poor bloke, fighting off his jet lag and boredom whilst trying to break the Internet."

"And this actually is, for want of a better phrase, the nub of the issue."

Jamie looked surprised. He hadn't considered for a second that Roops actually had a point to make, let alone a serious one. He thought he was just having one of his moments.

Roops continued. "For the occasional traveller, who's looking for that short escape from their home life and enjoying some personal space, sampling restaurants alone or even having complete power of the TV remote control, being in a little hotel room once in a while is absolutely fine. It's possibly even quite refreshing."

"For the regular business traveller, it is the absolute depth of despair. It is the point which brings home exactly how shit this particular way of life is. This is not a job of fun Jamie."

"True, getting up at 4.30am and battling your way through and past people just to do your job, just to get from A to B, is frustrating, irritating and occasionally throws up the odd opportunity for humour."

"But it's that first moment when you step into the small, characterless hotel room that it slams home to you that you are completely and utterly alone."

"Again."

Roops said the word, as if slamming it down on the table in front of him.

"Just like last night, just like last week, just like next week will be too."

"And on a very serious note, that can be depressing. I know people Jamie who have gone completely off the rails with this life. They are functioning and not so functioning alcoholics because they've got nothing better to do with the boring nights."

"The depression and the dread also begins to creep backwards, into the day itself. As you sit at your desk in the office watching everyone else leaving to go home to their family, you know that you're heading back to an empty, soulless hotel room."

"Again" said Roops with a similar emphasis as before.

"Just like last night, just like last week and just like the countless number of times in the future."

Jamie started to get worried about where this was going.

Roops carried on.

"Before you even travel, you are thinking about it – dreading it. You resent the fact that you're getting up at a ridiculous hour for very little thanks and even less acknowledgement. Allegedly, it's because you're in a position of trust and privilege that you get to do this."

"That's like telling someone that they can pay for the drinks all night because they're the most responsible. It's not a compliment – it's a pain."

"You know that you're going to be sat in front of inane television shows, shows you would never contemplate watching in your own home, because there's nothing else worthwhile to do. You've done all the interesting stuff before, when being away was still a novelty."

"Some people sit and do more work. But this job isn't about working 16 hours a day - you'd kill yourself! Nobody can work that long every single day and be productive. It's just not possible so don't kid yourself."

"You call home to speak to your family and it's like looking down on them from another planet - heaven even - with you in some strange parallel universe, and them carrying on with a normal life that you're not part of. They remember you exist but your call is merely an interruption to their own well-established routine."

By this point, Roops didn't even seem to be talking to Jamie, staring into space instead.

"Your health begins to suffer as you seek solace in junk and comfort food and of course, alcohol. From sampling local eateries with your £35 nightly food budget in the early days, you now resort to a bottle of wine from the local Tesco Metro washed down with crisps, peanuts and chocolate for dessert. Occasionally you break the mould and get some chicken drumsticks - because greasy fingers in a hotel room are just so appealing."

Jamie sat in stony silence. He'd never thought of Roops being so open about anything. Was this a confessional? Was it a warning?

"Sleeping then becomes more and more broken. Far from the luxury of being swept away in a sea of dreams as Lenny Henry would have you believe in his Premier Inn adverts, you're now in a cycle of dozing off to then awaken every hour, on the hour from 2am."

"Since attempting to sleep has now become too much of a struggle, you turn on the television to watch a rerun of Countdown or Deal or No Deal. Watching Noel Edmonds at 4am is no way to live your life Jamie."

"If that doesn't work, and your neighbour hasn't completely broken the hotel WiFi with his viewing habits, you go on the internet for a while. All the while, messing with your head."

"You blame the air conditioning unit, a relatively new addition to hotels like these, for the extremely variable and arbitrary heat settings that it seems to make up as it goes along. But in reality, the problem lies a lot deeper."

"By morning, you look and feel ten times worse than you did the previous day when you at least had the excuse of battling through the morning rush hour after being up since 4.30am to fly down."

"You don't think straight all day, your words don't come out in the right order and you're more irritable than usual. You're basically a mess. You lose motivation to snap out of this cycle. The gym holds no appeal, healthy living even less."

"Sometimes you go out for dinner with other colleagues or even for a business function. These are mere diversions from facing the stark reality of why you're there in the first place – all the anger, frustration and criticism that you throw out at the world on your journey is masking the truth."

"You're depressed with your life, its worth and with the fact that the value you allegedly bring to an organisation boils down to you needing to spend time alone, away from the people you want to be with most in the world, sat inside a grey and white Ikea-like box."

"It's a compromise that's needed to continue with the life and comforts you have at home – which in itself makes it all the harder."

"Jeez Roops, this is a bit heavy" said Jamie not quite knowing where to look. "Does an American Hot always bring this side out in you?"

"Nah, you're right. I just sometimes sit and reflect on it all maybe a bit too much …"

"Maybe a lot too much" interjected Jamie …

"Well, not so quick. It's really important to know that if you choose to embark on this life, it's not a bed of roses. It's not great. It can be very lonely and more than a bit shit. You sometimes have to find ways to amuse yourself. These emails I write are me trying to keep myself entertained. I know they're probably harmless and that nobody will ever read them but the important thing for me is they allow some escapism from where I am, who I am and what I'm meant to exist for."

"London brings to life the diverse nature of society meaning you never fail to appreciate the cosseted life that you have. You never take it for granted and wouldn't change it for the world. You don't resent "it", the job, the circumstances and all that, because you accept it for what it is. It's the price you pay. It's just sometimes a high price to pay."

Jamie took time to reflect on this.

It was quite sobering, he thought. He'd always imagined that there would have been a lot more fun being away from home.

"So what you're saying Roops, if I've picked you up correctly, is that most of these City hotels are occupied each night with thoroughly depressed individuals, addicted to prawn cocktail crisps who have a penchant for excessive masturbation?"

"Ha ha!! Spot on Jamie!! Ha! I suppose so, although the crisps don't have to be prawn cocktail …"

Jamie would never look at anyone else in the hotel breakfast room in quite the same way! Poor Roops he thought. He'd never really considered the impact this job had on him. And addicted to prawn cocktail crisps too??

"Let's lift the mood a bit Roops. You must have written an email to someone about staying in a shit hotel room or being away from home or something like that? I love reading your emails - let me see one?"

"Oh all right then. I don't like sharing ..." said Roops, flattered by the attention these were getting.

"Bollocks you don't ...!" belted back Jamie.

"My favourite one was this one here. I wrote it to the CEO of Tesco Metro. Ha ha!! I even suggest criminal activity - purely for social and economic purposes of course!"

"Fantastic! Give it here!" whooped Jamie.

Roops's suggested email to the CEO of Tesco Metro:

"Dear Sir or Madam,

I am a regular user of your stores when travelling to London for short stays. I like the ease and simplicity of them however I'd like to offer some thoughts which I think might improve the experience for me, a typical business traveller.

My main purpose, and I suspect it's the same for many people like me, for using your stores is to purchase food for the evening I have ahead in my hotel room. That means, I need simple foods that don't require a microwave to cook them nor utensils to eat them.

So I don't really need your soups. It's just too complicated to contemplate how I could successfully eat them (although I appreciate a cleverly packaged gazpacho might tempt me).

I do like variety and my diet needs to remain focused on reflecting the mood that I'm in at that point in time. This means I tend to search out crisps (all varieties), peanuts (all varieties), chocolate (all varieties) and occasionally a stodgy sandwich. And of course, some white wine.

So I'm finding that I waste precious minutes trying to search out these items because you scatter them around the four corners of your store. That's not very helpful at all. That means that whilst I'm searching for my favourite prawn cocktail crisps, I'm using up valuable time I could otherwise be spending staring at my bedroom walls.

Can I suggest that rather than categorising your sections in the traditional way of Snacks, Confectionary, Alcohol etc you just cut to the chase and have one area entitled "All You Will Want to Eat Tonight Mr Businessman"? It would save us all so much time and effort.

I'd be in and out in a flash, you'd increase your sales per minute ratio and given the general laziness of those using it, you could even throw some stock in there which is past its "Sell By" date. No one would ever notice.

If you put together packages of food and wine, it would also reduce the need for any further decision making on the part of your shoppers, which after lots of travelling and a long hard day is the last thing many of us need. Just pull together a selection of crisps, nuts, chocolate and wine for a single price and you'd be off and running. Just follow the mantra "stodge is good" and you can't go wrong.

Finally, and I appreciate that some might consider this slightly illegal, but you could consider inflating the prices of everything in this section to cover the cost of some Marlboro Lights?

That way, I could purchase my "London fags" within my daily subsistence allowance but ensure they're not recorded on any receipt? You could even keep some extra profit back for yourself. It'd be a great little earner for us both - bordering on genius actually.

If you want to discuss this, or any of my other business ideas, please get in touch.

Best, as ever,

Yours faithfully

Rupert X Wardhaugh"

Chapter 16
Let's Dance

Staring across at Jamie in the pizza restaurant, Roops couldn't help but notice the efforts he'd gone to for what was basically two blokes sitting in some completely soulless restaurant in the City of London, surrounded by other business people in exactly the same position as them.

"You've changed" said Roops, in an almost accusing manner.

"What do you mean "I've changed" responded Jamie deliberately missing the point "You barely knew me before and now you're saying I've sold out or something?"

"No, no - calm down. Your clothes, you've changed to come out this evening," said Roops. "You've gone to some effort too. Is that satin on that shirt??"

"Get lost, of course it's not satin! It's a sort of fake silk bit of detail … Why?? Does it matter?" said Jamie, now getting very defensive.

Roops starting chuckling "Of course it doesn't. It's just a lot of effort, all that extra room and weight added to your luggage bag. I wouldn't do it anymore unless I have an official thing to attend and even then … I stopped bringing my kilt years ago because it was just too heavy with all the crap you have to bring with it. And it's way too hot to wear in these old hotels with no air conditioning."

"Well, I like to make a bit of an effort Roops. I quite like the feeling of shedding my work clothes, and then showering, to freshen up for the night. It gives me the feeling of drawing a line under the work day. It's almost a ceremonial part of the day for me.

"And it means I get to play my "Getting Ready" song …"

"Hang on! Hang right on there sunshine … Your what?! Your 'Getting what'!?" laughed Roops, his eyes wide open with incredulity.

"Oh come on Roops - you must know what I mean? Surely everybody has a "Getting Ready" song? Surely?"

For Jamie, the "Getting Ready" song had become a central part of his evening preparations – his perfectly legal drug of choice, his adrenaline boosting, caffeine replacing, shot in the arm steroid, his heartbeat-spiking, burst of energy. He could now never prepare to go out at night without this vital part of the process. The night was simply doomed to failure otherwise.

His whole set up became one long ritual, almost militaristic to the point that he was bordering on OCD with it.

With his portable speaker linked through Bluetooth to his iPhone, he'd select a song with an appropriately jaunty beat with which he would then perform the most bizarre routine designed to "get him going" for whatever lay ahead.

He'd start by standing in front of the bathroom mirror cleaning his teeth, waving his arse from side to side trying to sing (with a toothbrush in his mouth) whilst busting some mega shapes.

Then, his moves would have to become a little less erratic as he shaved, either in the traditional sense around his face or perhaps even whilst performing some delicate "manscaping", for fear of serious injury.

But once that was out of the way, he'd be rocking.

His moves would become more pronounced and he'd really start to exaggerate his steps. He'd be thinking to himself "Yeah, you've got rhythm man", as if he had been lifted straight from the floor of The Soul Train studios.

He had a serious dose of attitude with some funk sprinkled on top for good measure as he strutted through every bar of his chosen song with the confirmed poise of a 1970s dude.

His previously undiscovered talent for singing would unleash itself as he steps into the shower, the introduction of shampoo and shower gel acting as an additional accoutrement to his routine, the acoustics of the bathroom seeming to suit his voice perfectly. "My god" he would think "why did I never pursue that singing career?"

As he moves around the shower, his body will sway from side to side, the spray of the shower hitting the surrounding walls and curtain replicating the sound of a tightened snare drum, the water dancing in perfect cadence.

He's now towel drying himself – man, he is the coolest cat as he cavorts in front of the full length mirror weaving through to the bedroom to start dressing. His moves are so with it.

Each addition of clothing deserves an ever more pronounced rhythmic burst or thrust – until he gets to his shoes. (There's not really any way that a pair of sturdy brogues can be put on with panache or flamboyance. It just can't be done. It's all down to physics apparently.)

He'd finish by gazing admiringly at the finished article in front of him. "People are going to gasp as you walk through the door later" he'd say to himself "that moment will be yours and you're going to smash it!"

Thank God nobody was there to witness any of this. For his sake.

———————-

"I've never heard of such a thing!" said Roops. "I sometimes have the TV on in the background, Countdown maybe or just the news but … I feel I'm going to regret this, do you have any particular "Getting Ready" song Jamie? A bit of Hi-NRG perhaps?" asked Roops, nervous to where this conversation was heading.

"No, not one in particular, it changes all the time. My dad was really into his music and so I grew up with a huge variety playing constantly. I've ended up with really diverse tastes," said Jamie earnestly. This was something he clearly took very seriously thought Roops.

For Jamie, this was his moment to really impress Roops. This was more than just throwing "Ealing comedies" into the conversation for effect - this stuff was his point of proper validation. Cavorting around his room naked to a 70s' soul tune was his chance to finally be taken seriously.

"It's difficult to pin it down to one tune in particular, especially when I have a boredom threshold so low that it drags along the floor behind me like a surly teenager!" he laughed. "And of course, being such an artiste of dance it's important to shake things up a bit to stay fresh."

Roops was now lost completely. He had all sorts of images flashing through his head at this point, some of them worryingly close to the truth of what went on in Jamie's bedroom before a night out.

Jamie pulled out his iPhone and looked up the iTunes app.

"Here we go, here's my current "Getting Ready" playlist. It needs to be on shuffle so this is in no particular order:

- Mr Blue Sky - ELO
- Love On Top - Beyonce
- Boys Keep Swinging - Bowie (Outside Tour '95)
- On My Radio – The Selecter
- Rapper's Delight – The Sugarhill Gang (not the 14 minute version)
- Baby, I Love You – The Ramones
- Flashing Lights – Kanye West
- Avenues and Alleyways – Tony Christie
- Superstition - Stevie Wonder
- This Town Ain't Big Enough for the Both of Us - Sparks
- Headstart for Happiness – The Style Council
- Blackberry Way – The Move
- Groove Is In The Heart - Deee-Lite
- Telephone – Lady Gaga
- State of Independence - Donna Summer
- Human – The Killers
- Dracula - Basement Jaxx
- Love Train - The O'Jays
- Black Betty - Ram Jam
- I Bet You Look Good On The Dancefloor – Arctic Monkeys
- Ten Tonne Skeleton – Royal Blood
- Shaft – Isaac Hayes
- Galvanize - The Chemical Brothers
- Downtown – Macklemore & Ryan Lewis
- Midnight Train To Georgia - Gladys Knight and The Pips

"Wow!" said Roops, seriously impressed. "No Taylor Swift though. And I'm sorry, but I was expecting at least something by The Proclaimers!"

"No, no, no" jumped in Jamie. He sat up readying to make what to him was a very serious point of order.

"There is absolutely never, ever any room or place on my "Getting Ready" playlist for the "Ant and Dec" of the Scottish music scene. As far as I'm concerned, they were last seen singing about an alleged appearance of the sun somewhere over the empty expanses of Easter Road stadium which is where they're best left. Imagine singing that the sun would ever shine on that shower…!"

Another tick in the box for Roops - Jamie was clearly a lover of expansive and passing football favoured by the team on the western side of the Capital city. None of the ego-inflating "hoof-ball" that the little team in the east played out every week.

"And Taylor Swift's alright by the way. She was on the list until recently but I always keep it strictly to 25 songs at a time and the Sugarhill Gang bumped her off the list."

"And in case you're wondering, this whole "Getting Ready" routine never happens in the morning - I'd never make it out of the house …"

Roops just sat and laughed.

"Brilliant" he said, with genuine warmth. "Right, I can't take anymore excitement, I'm going to call it a night now. By the way, I don't do hotel breakfasts, so I'll just see you in the office tomorrow? And at least were flying back - none of that train malarkey. Being all uphill the train takes so much longer …"

Jamie sat thinking that one through, the fog of beer for a second making him actually believe that London to Edinburgh was actually "all up hill".

The following morning Roops awoke thinking about the previous evening and whether he could ever have a "Getting Ready" song, let alone an entire playlist. But at least he'd quite enjoyed the various chats with Jamie, it turned out that he was a good listener which for someone as egocentric as Roops made him the perfect companion.

One thing was certain in Roops's mind. Even if he did have a 'Getting Ready' song, it would never be used on the last day of a business trip no matter how much he saw getting home as a cause for celebration.

Chapter 17
Where Are We Now?

The day to return home should bring some light relief after all that's gone on already this week but Roops was never quite dancing down the street, splashing and kicking through puddles in a Gene Kelly type of way.

The light at the end of the tunnel – his home - should provide an air of positivity. It means sleeping in his own bed, friendly company in the evening, a balanced diet and a much better all round environment. At the very least, it represented a familiarity that he was happy to have.

But deep down, as Roops checked out of his hotel in the morning he had a heavy heart and an air of resignation because not only did he have to face another journey just to get home – which potentially could be much worse than the one coming down – he also knew that the whole thing will be repeated again in less than a week's time.

This trip had gone relatively smoothly, much better than he had ever thought it would if he was being truthful. He had Jamie to thank in no small way for that. Jamie had at least lifted the boredom and Roops had to concede that he quite enjoyed having someone around for companionship.

But the pessimist in Roops, or as he would say the realist, recognised that having a good trip this time meant that the law of averages would be waiting to screw him over next time – a flight cancellation, delays, fog bound airports, the very worst hotels or worse, an apart-hotel thing. Next time could be or would be, much worse.

But before he even gets to that, he still has to get today out of the way first. By this point in the trip, he's knackered after a few days facing all sorts of hurdles and irritations and with potentially more hurdles to overcome.

He'd again been less than healthy probably having at least two more beers with Jamie than he should have, he'd barely slept and he could swear that cats were following him down the street, drawn to the pungent smells emanating from the unwashed, sweaty clothes in his travel case.

The rest of the day would be spent sitting in meetings with one eye on the clock. There is absolutely no way that any meeting can overrun. All Roops wants is the person in front of him to break the habit of a lifetime and get to the point and be succinct. Of course, luck will inevitably curse him once again and the people he meets invariably turn out to be like a Pink Floyd record – things that can be said in three minutes will almost certainly take 15.

Roops became more and more agitated as the day wore on because he knew how much time he needs to walk to the DLR, through the ticket barriers and down to the platform, then in turn allow for a train journey of roughly 25 minutes to get him down to the airport in enough time to avoid any last minute and embarrassing rushes through security.

Roops and Jamie had the benefit of flying home with BA, who at least have a good app which lets travellers stay relatively well-informed of whether the flight should be on time – certainly better informed than when you're physically at the airport. That at least gives you some comfort around their ability to honour their side of the bargain later.

For what is a relatively simple thing to have, Roops would get frustrated that the other airlines didn't at least try to do the same thing. But then again, he thought, their ability to predict potential departure times are hindered by their choice of aircraft and the fact that they seem so temperamental at the slightest sign of a cloud in the sky!

Roops emotions surrounding this leg of his journey were of course different but still gave him plenty of reason to moan, complain and pick fault. His initial outbound journey was based on need with the very purpose of his professional life meaning that he'd had to be at the final destination, at a certain time, preferably in as calm a mood as possible.

Most people's companies would feel the same about this point he reckoned. After all, they would want you to be performing at your very best, having picked you to do the role based on your abilities. Roops would argue that it would be counter-intuitive if you were hindered by continued frustrations and obstructions brought on by a cost-consciousness which became counterproductive.

But yet a poor travelling experience can have precisely that impact with all your stresses and frustrations borne from the fact that you just needed, and wanted to do your job but couldn't either because you had been forced to use cheaper options or worse, the infrastructure wouldn't work as intended.

Needless to say, Roops had this well thought through, probably constructed as he was standing in yet another queue of delayed passengers.

"We all like to be seen in a positive light but we're not always giving ourselves the best opportunity to do so" he would say.

But the return leg of his journey had a different dynamic because Roops just really, really wanted to get home. By this point, he'd had enough of the business trip and he couldn't wait just to tumble through his front door, get out of his work clothes and into a pair of shorts and find out what's been going on whilst he'd been away.

Over lunch, Roops decided to give Jamie some advice on the topic of travelling home which was far from a straightforward subject. There were many pitfalls to consider and it shouldn't be assumed that the PAs in the office nor the travel company had any clue on the matter.

Listening to this advice was in no way optional for Jamie to hear, this lesson instead now being part of Roops new found ambition to become Yoda to Jamie's Luke Skywalker.

"We're travelling home from City airport and that's not by accident. The airport that you choose to get home from, like the journey down, plays an important part in the success of your trip," he started, talking close to a whisper as if this was some secret which could only be trusted in the hands of a few chosen ones.

"I've given this a lot of thought over the years. You need to take into account several factors in order to maximise success:
1. How easy is it to get to the airport from central London?
2. How long will it take to get to the said airport?
3. What airlines use this airport?
4. What is the airport predominantly used for?
5. How susceptible to weather conditions is this airport?"

"You need to consider each point carefully because each one can have an impact on your journey and consequently, your sanity."

"Firstly though, there is one rule which stands true no matter the answer to any of these five questions. That is, if you choose to fly home from Gatwick having been in central London, then frankly you deserve everything that is thrown at you on the trip."

"God, you've really got a thing about Gatwick Roops!" said Jamie "Were you scarred there as a child or something??"

"No, no - don't get me wrong. This isn't a dig at Gatwick per se. Gatwick as an airport tries really hard and has of course created its own brilliant little niche as the world's first "Retro Airport". The problem is its location and the people in charge of getting you to it from central London."

"Remember, to get to Gatwick, there is a very good chance that you need to place your complete trust and faith in the hands of Southern Rail but that's like handing your child to Rose West for babysitting duties or handing someone a hand grenade with the pin pulled out."

"It'll be some time before I can forget about Gatwick and the trains Roops!" laughed Jamie.

"Well, if you're going to Gatwick, you're presumably going to catch a flight which means you would have to hope that on that particular day, someone in Southern Rail has read the timetable and have made some semblance of an effort to try to get their trains where they need to be and at the right time that they need to be. But all evidence would suggest that they're not very good at either of those things."

"Southern Rail appear to spend so long working out how they can put their fares up that they forget that there's a long queue of passengers outside their window waiting on them to switch their giant train set on. Historically they used to create pricing structures so confusing that by the time you'd worked out the cheapest priced ticket combination, you'd probably have missed the train altogether."

"Now, they just cut to the chase and are quite up front with their price increases - they don't even appear to be that embarrassed by it."

"To be fair, they've reduced the chances of you missing the train because most of the time Southern Rail trains are either running late or just not bothering to run at all. Southern Rail trains appear to take duvet days – so if you rely on them to get you to your plane on time, then you are taking a very big chance. It's like dangling your legs in a swimming pool in the middle of a lightning storm – you're just asking for trouble."

"The challenge Gatwick airport has is that in an ideal world, it would move to a different location. But that's quite a tricky thing to do, all of which is a shame for Gatwick …"

"I think we've been here before Roops …?" ventured Jamie hoping against hope that he wasn't about to suffer another lengthy monologue.

"You have absolutely nothing disparaging to say about Gatwick. It's just Southern Rail you don't like …" offered Jamie.

"Not just me, there are 300,000 travellers every day who hate them! I'm in a club which has more members than the One Direction fan club!! And that pun is intended - people who rely on Southern Rail are in the "No Direction" fan club!!" laughed Roops.

"Anyway, you're putting me off my stride. This is important for your future career as a business traveller …"

"I never thought my career was being a business traveller, Roops …?"

"No, you wouldn't. It will get dressed up with a fancy title like Relationship Manager or Account Director, but you'll actually just be a professional traveller. And it's shit. Well paid shit, which is the good thing, but shit all the same."

"Don't dress it up for me then!" roared Jamie.

"So …" said Roops, eyebrows raising slightly like a bookish schoolteacher urging his class to return to concentrating on the lesson at hand.

"Heathrow is a little better because it at least has the excellent Heathrow Express. Apart from the fact that you need to take out a second mortgage to travel on it, and you need to clamber over the most enormous suitcases that people insist on travelling with just to find a seat, it generally gets you to Heathrow in good time. Which is a good thing."

"The Heathrow Express trains try to create a certain ambience recognising that travelling isn't the best thing to be doing. The carriages are modern and the train even has video presentations playing in the carriages to keep you amused, although the news loop seems to be mostly out of date or at least, running late. I spent one trip thinking that Nelson Mandela had died for a second time until I realised what was going on."

Jamie laughed not knowing whether this was a serious point or not. Roops had a dry sense of humour which at times confused the hell out of him.

"Have you ever been to T5 yet Jamie?" asked Roops, continuing before Jamie had a chance to respond. "It has a pretty good Check

In area with a Fast Track queue through security to quicken up the process or keep you away from holidaymakers – it's all a matter of your perspective, which works in its favour."

"The problem Heathrow has if you're coming from the City, is that you need to travel some distance using different means before you start "their" process. To put it a different way, you need to get the Central Line from Bank tube station to Lancaster Gate. And that's far from fun. In fact, it's as much fun as a chip pan fire – and probably hotter."

"Ouch!" chuckled Jamie.

"Yeah, you see the Central Line is basically one giant furnace designed to drain you of all the bodily fluids capable of seeping through your sweat glands in as short a time as possible. If you can imagine running a marathon through the Sahara desert but fully dressed in one of those comedy charity outfits – the divers outfit springs to mind – then that's what travelling on the Central Line is like. It's like being inside a tumble dryer. I came off it one day and my suit had shrunk around my body! I looked like Alexei Sayle …" said Roops, completely deadpan.

"And on top of that, its route also goes through Oxford Circus and Bond Street which are probably two of the busiest parts of London for tourists. And I don't even need to go into detail about what that means. I'll just leave you with one word – stench. The stenchiest stench of all stenches. It stinks."

"Yep, got it - it's hot and smelly …" interjected Jamie joining in.

"Yeah, well these things are important. So whilst Heathrow has lots going for it once you get there, it's a bugger to get to if you're starting from the City."

"And so to cut to the chase, I won't even bother going into Luton or Stansted. They can wait for another day when you're more tolerant ..." Roops said cheekily.

"London City Airport stands head and shoulders above all the others, in my opinion for the first four factors but is incredibly exposed to number five."

"When London City airport works, it works brilliantly. Of course, it's not perfect and it has faced some issues, but let's face it, getting to 100% perfect is probably an unrealistic expectation."

"Because the airport is serviced by the DLR, which has stations situated in the City, and with a journey time of only twenty minutes, getting to London City Airport is very easy. The DLR is mostly above ground meaning you have the unique and pleasant sensation of clean air, by London standards, wafting in at every stop."

"If you're really lucky you get to see that most rare of sights on London's transport network – an empty seat. I saw one once but decided not to try it for fear it was actually a mirage."

"Because of its location and the ease of getting to it, you don't need to use up half of your day just to get to City Airport. That's way more efficient and reduces the chances of something going wrong. It also means using other forms of transport, say a taxi or Uber, if pushed isn't completely unfeasible or ridiculously overpriced."

"But it's when you reach the airport that it comes into its own. London City Airport is mostly used by business travellers or, as I'm often told, PLUs. That's "People Like Us" apparently! Who makes up these terms!?" he laughed.

"My girlfriend mostly" said Jamie dryly.

"Now, this is in no way meant to be a social comment nor a condescending judgement of non-business travellers …" started Roops

"Yeah right" laughed Jamie "That means that you're about to be condescending to non-business travellers!"

"No, what I'm meaning is that factually, most of the people using City airport are business travellers who fly regularly and as such, know what to do and what is expected. They know that security needs you to remove all belts and coats. They know that you should put laptops in a separate tray and that you can only have one bag of toiletries containing items each less than 100mls. They generally have one item of hand luggage and mostly, they don't try to take the piss," defended Roops.

With a sense of triumphalism, he then declared "In fact, London City airport must have the most compliant set of passengers of any UK airport," before returning to form by saying "If it weren't for the fact that the airport security process itself is at times a complete disaster. Its security system is sometimes so inept that you'd think they'd handed the keys to people who are on a job swap from Southern Trains. Otherwise it's perfect."

"But all of this is trifling because fundamentally, you're at the airport to get on a plane which then takes you home. And that's when City Airport's Achilles heel comes into play …" said Roops adopting a tone to imply some impending drama.

"I said earlier that when City Airport works, it works brilliantly. On the other hand, when it doesn't work, it grinds to a shuddering halt and it feels like this happens here more than at any other airport. This might have something to do with the vicinity of high buildings on its landing path or maybe it's in an area more susceptible to variable weather. Maybe its runway length has an impact if the weather is inclement. It might have something to do with the technology on board some of the planes that use it."

"I'm not actually sure but whatever the reason, London City Airport can and does grind to a halt more often than others and that causes chaos. Until recently, the airport itself couldn't cope with an increasing number of people flooding into its departure area to sit and wait on flights that were never going to take off."

"It was pretty awful to be fair particularly when you consider how much people were paying to fly from there. You would find yourself standing staring at screens, whilst struggling to find a little corner of a shelf or pillar to lean against listening in to fellow passengers conversations. They mostly seem to be Dutch people or sometimes Swiss."

"None of them Swedish though Roops! They're probably all at home having their washing machines fixed I'll bet!" laughed Jamie referring to the previous evening's conversation about hotel habits.

"Ha ha! Exactly! No wonder the chef in the Muppet Show was always smiling!" smirked Roops.

"Finnish ..."

"All right, all right, I'm getting to the point ..."

"No, wasn't the chef in The Muppet Show Finnish? From Finland ...??"

"No way! Don't you know anything? The chef in The Muppet Show was definitely Swedish ... get your phone out and Google it. £10 says I'm right ... and another £10 for spoiling my joke you little fucker ... Tour forfeits count on business trips too you know!"

"Mmm. OK, I'll take your word for it ..." said Jamie, not entirely believing it. But he did reflect that he'd never felt such warmth in being called a "little fucker" before!

Roops it turns out was of course 100% correct which he took to reminding Jamie about regularly. "Don't argue with Uncle Rupert" he would say patronisingly at every opportunity for the rest of the day "Remember what happened last time ...?"

Sensing Jamie had completely lost interest in his theory of "the best airport to fly home from" Roops quickly summed up that City was now a bit bigger and had more food and drink options. Meaning that one of his biggest gripes no longer existed (although he didn't specifically concede that there was one less thing for him to moan about).

"And which of these various targets have had an email written about them?" asked Jamie.

"The Central Line, of course" responded Roops. "It's awful. I wrote this one with the phone almost sliding out of my sweat ridden palms ..."

"Dear Sir or Madam,

When I was growing up, I wanted to be the most popular boy in my school. Being devoid of any social skills, I would force my parents to host lavish parties to create the impression of a popularity that would make Silvio Berlusconi blush.

This has carried in to my adult life where I shamelessly pursue friends through social media befriending anyone who shows even a passing interest in what I'm up to. The result is a bulging Inbox of comments from people who don't know me nor have ever even met me. I can't actually cope with it but that's not the point.

I couldn't help thinking that if the Central Line were a living person it would be like that. It feels like it just wants to keep hoovering up passengers – friends – at every opportunity irrespective of whether it can cope.

It's the most narcissistic of the Tube lines on your network and it needs to learn that it's not about how many people it can take on board but the quality of the experience and engagement it can provide.

I think it's seriously close to a breakdown - do you think you should have a word with it?

Yours faithfully,

Rupert X Wardhaugh"

"Roops, this sounds like some kind of confessional!" laughed Jamie. "Please just reconfirm that you don't actually send these emails out?"

"No, no, I just do them to keep my mind busy and occupied. I think if I did send them I'd probably end up getting a knock on the door at midnight from some unsavoury character threatening to put me in my place ..."

"You still owe me £20 Jamie. I've not forgotten …" Roops barked, trying to break the sombre mood. "And by the way, don't be thinking you've just climbed Brokeback Mountain … ha ha!"

Chapter 18
Unwashed and Somewhat Slightly Dazed

Roops really enjoyed returning home from any journey but this one was especially nice since not only was he flying on his favoured airline, this evening also had one of his favourite cabin crew working on it, the always brilliant Gail Brown.

Roops felt some relief when she was leading the crew because she stands head and shoulders above most of the others. Seeing her at the top of the plane steps gave him comfort that from here on, things were going to be ok.

Some cabin crew can be quite dismissive as if the passengers are just an inconvenience to their day - Gail at least recognises the regulars and greets them like old friends (and gives them extra wine if she's in a really good mood). Which is really nice. It sort of feels a bit old school - how flying and great service should work hand in hand.

Similarly, when finally landing back at his "own" airport he felt a feeling of comfort, as if his own mother's arms were being wrapped around him in a big warm hug. He always took a moment to take in that first burst of fresh air which immediately calmed him - he barely needed to even open his eyes to know that he'd returned to his home city.

The chatter all around him mirrored accents and colloquialisms that he'd known all his life, faces everywhere like old acquaintances. It was a very strange experience to explain.

The people to whom he had been so openly sneering when he left on his journey had suddenly become like siblings to him. He had a sense of comfort and familiarity with everything he encountered.

Getting out of the terminal appeared to be a lot less frustrating too than it was when he was arriving for a flight. The obstructions he faced from holidaymakers on the way in now didn't seem to exist. Most people appeared to be sitting chatting over a civilised glass of wine or maybe even a coffee, children were playing nicely on the climbing frames and there feels a calmness to the airport. Strangely, most passengers even seem to be walking mostly in straight lines.

On this latest return home, Roops wandered down the Exit stairs from the Departure hall, relieved that this particular journey was nearly all over. But then a final shadow fell over him.

Jamie's luggage had been put in the hold and Roops felt a responsibility to stay with his fellow traveller to the bitter end despite Jamie's protestations.

Roops had enjoyed having Jamie with him and felt a kind of paternal instinct towards him.

Jamie for his part felt a bit stupid that his bag had ended up being taken from him, blaming the constantly changing rules around hand luggage sizes which he felt were becoming more and more deliberately vague, something that Roops naturally had sympathy with.

Jamie hadn't been naive. He knew the basic rules which were reasonably fair and consistent - all liquids had to fit in the small plastic bag and individually be no more than 100ml. This was a rule which is widely known to most people who display even the slightest bit of consciousness and ability to concentrate on a television news item for longer than 20 seconds ("meaning the new security rules remain a complete mystery to most people flying on Jet2 to Marbella" he thought).

If Roops heard Jamie's complaint once though, he heard it at least 10 times when they were sitting in the Departure Lounge of City airport.

"The airlines are really just taking the complete piss and using the whole concept of luggage as another reason to squeeze extra cash from the poor traveller," moaned Jamie.

"I wish they'd make their bloody minds up. There's no consistency of rule around what's an acceptable size of hand luggage! That means it's virtually impossible to have one case which caters for several days away which is acceptable to all the airlines. So that means that invariably you're almost certainly going to have to put your bag in the hold for an extra £45 at some point! It's racketeering!"

Roops had wanted to point out to him that they were at least flying BA, which is probably the most liberal of all the airlines when it comes to hand luggage, however he suspected Jamie was in no mood to listen.

It would mean that Jamie would have to admit that he'd fucked up altogether on his choice of case for his stay meaning he'd further have to admit he was still wet around the ears for bringing a change of clothes for the previous evening's pizza … and even Roops couldn't skewer him like that, not right now anyway. He'd probably leave that for when they were all back in the office and he had an audience to properly satisfy his pleasure in that moment!

Jamie's mood hadn't lightened in the slightest by the time they reached the baggage carousel.

"How difficult is it to get a bag off a plane and onto a moving belt?" he complained. "There's not really too much that can go wrong on short flights with no connections surely? They can't have lost it!"

"I just want to get home. I've spent the last few days away wearing the same shoes in all that time. I feel like I'm walking like a First World War veteran with trench foot. I feel like I've been in this suit for days - it's now sticking to me in the most inappropriate places and I've spent the last day walking around London dragging that bloody oversized trolley case at my back! I smell clammy and sweaty, I haven't had enough sleep and my mouth is basically minging. My lips feel like little fly traps constantly sticking to my teeth and my breath is so bad that even I can smell it myself."

"I just dream of getting home, into a hot shower with a fully charged electric toothbrush in my hand!"

"Aye, aye tiger!" Roops burst out laughing and had to look in the other direction.

"What are you finding so funny? It's OK for you with your little carry on case, all smug because you know what you're doing."

"I know, I know, I'm sorry," said Roops apologetically before adding "By the way, when was it you said your period was due?"

Roops turned away and let out the most enormous laugh delighting in the misery of his travel companion. Jamie had to laugh at himself now. He really was being pathetic.

The last hour of the trip - the flight - was, they thought, the final hurdle to overcome. But now both Jamie and Roops found themselves trying to decipher the secret code laid in front of them by Edinburgh airport baggage control namely, guess which belt your bag will arrive on and more importantly, when?

Sitting on a plane for an hour, stinking, is no fun but it's a holiday compared to standing next to a baggage belt for another hour staring up at a small television screen waiting for your bag to be returned.

"Do you know that we've spent just as long waiting on my poxy bag as we did up in the air on the plane? In other words, although it was on exactly the same plane as us, my bag has taken twice as long to get to its destination as we did. And I paid an extra £45 for that to happen!" complained Jamie.

Every so often they would both hear a distant rumble which they thought was the small battery operated truck pulling metal cages towards the corrugated iron door at the mouth of the belt. Each time their hopes were raised only to come crashing down as a different belt in the Arrivals Hall jolted into action.

"Have you ever seen one?" asked Jamie.

"Seen what" replied Roops, slightly confused as to where this was going.

"A baggage handler. You never see them but you can hear their footsteps. But it's weird, because you never hear them having a conversation like you would other workers. I've never known two painters to remain quiet when they're at work - they're either always talking or whistling along to the tunes on their radio. But these baggage handlers never seem to talk to each other. The only thing you ever hear is the noise of bags being thrown and occasionally drop kicked towards a belt."

Roops smiled in agreement. "Yeah, it's a good point. They must be freezing out there mind you - it's always cold on airport tarmacs."

Jamie was in no mood to concede anything to them though and just stared back at Roops.

"Did you bring your car with you?" asked Jamie, eager to move the conversation to a different topic as they waited for his bag.

"Well two things there Jamie."

"Number one. Unless I've recently won the lottery, or our company has such poor financial controls that they're about to go bust, it's highly unlikely that you'll ever bring your car to the multistorey carpark because it is, quite frankly, absolutely extortionate. It is attempting to single-handedly fund not only the building of a new runway at Edinburgh but I suspect new runways at every other airport around the UK. I wouldn't be surprised if it has a GDP currently higher than Ireland and if it continues to generate cash at its current rate, it could consider launching its own currency and seek independence from the rest of the UK."

"OK. Point made. And number two?" ventured Jamie.

"We got the train down, you idiot, so I wouldn't have parked at the airport in any case" laughed Roops. "This is like shelling peas" he thought wearily.

"How were you planning to get home?" asked Roops half-heartedly.

"Probably the tram I reckon."

"Oh jeez, good luck with that. It's usually full of old folk at this time of day" said Roops, "I'll be ordering a company contract cab."

"And why will the tram be full of old folk?" said an equally weary Jamie.

The tram is a relatively new addition to Edinburgh and as with most new developments (the Scottish Parliament for example) it was not only controversial and massively over-budget but also became the number one talking point of every taxi driver and most of the incumbent citizens of Edinburgh over the age of 65. And they all, to a person, hated the idea of it.

The topic of the trams was to prove an enormous irritant to them but at the same time, a fantastic diversionary tactic for everyone else when conversations were taking a turn towards the duller end of the spectrum. Family gatherings, which invariably would revolve around the inane chatter of Aunt Ruby's latest issues with her varicose veins could immediately turn into a debate more vociferous and hostile than the Turks and the Greeks discussing the 1974 invasion of Cyprus. All you had to do was mention the word "Tram" with just a slightly positive lilt in your tone and everything kicked off.

Apparently, it was an enormous waste of money and nobody would use them. "They" would be better spending money on more parking spaces in the centre of town. "They" would be better off sorting out the huge traffic problems in the centre of town. And so on, and so on.

So Roops was by no means unique in having an opinion on the trams in that regard. But Jamie wagered his opinion would be different again.

Now that the tram system was up and running, what Roops had been referring to was that because pensioners get free travel, there are times when you can't get on one without making a prior booking through SAGA tours.

"All those old folk are taking day trips, out to the airport for coffee, cakes and a quick empty of their seeping colostomy bags." laughed Roops. "Suddenly the trams are a great idea! If you see my parents, say hello from me. They're never off the things."

"I just don't get the whole thing" he continued. "Over and above the enormous number of grey haired people and the consequent smell of stale urine on board, the tram still has some fundamental faults."

"Unlike every other major suburban tram network in the world, it only goes in a straight line into the City Centre. You try drawing the map of the London Underground from memory and it's pretty difficult if not impossible. For the Edinburgh tram system, you just need a ruler - not even a 12 inch ruler either because it doesn't go very far, a 6 inch one will do," he opined in an obviously well-rehearsed routine.

"Who in their right mind thought it would properly serve the people of the City? Because it's just on one line, it means that unless you live along that line - which only represents a small minority of the population of the City - this isn't going to be the best mode of transport for you."

"Or you could just be like me and get on a bus after I get off the tram in the city centre …" interjected Jamie.

Roops completely ignored this on the basis that in time, Jamie would be less altruistic in his approach to company expenses and end up in a taxi like everyone else.

He continued "OK, I concede that if you're a tourist looking to get into the City Centre for your hotel it works well assuming you can get a seat as a result of all the elderly people on board stuffed full of their Starbuck's cakes. But for the business traveller who lives in the suburbs, it doesn't work so well. They just want to get home as quickly and as directly as they can."

"And what is it with all the announcements you get? The tram has to have the most annoyingly repetitive announcements about its free WiFi on board! God, they're really chuffed with themselves with that thing - "free WiFi!" is being lauded as if the tram network was so pioneering that you'd think it was taking you straight to the heart of Silicon Valley itself. Next stop - Google! Ding Ding!!"

"Every two stops that female voice from the Marks & Spencer's advert crows away about them giving us free WiFi: "The net's on us ..." she sings! That really gets my goat that does! "Well my dear, without wanting to piss on your chips, it's actually "on us!"

"We, the business travellers and tourists, are the ones who have just paid £5 each way - a higher price than any other portion of the journey - on top of the enormous amount of public money spent on building this thing. So don't tell us that it's your generosity that's giving us free access to the internet! We paid for it all along!"

Thankfully for Jamie, at that point the flashing lights went on and a loud bleeping kicked in. "That sounds like a symphony to me" said Jamie relieved that at last, it sounded like his bag would finally be reunited with him. Admittedly they'd waited over an hour for this to happen but at least it was almost through and he wouldn't have to hear anymore stories from Roops.

It wasn't that he hadn't enjoyed their time, it was just that it had been a long two days and he was ready to pop.

He looked up and saw a sign proclaiming "Welcome to Scotland!" to which he added in his head, the footnote "We're treating you like shit from the minute you land!"

He turned to Roops and whined "It's as if we're attempting to be more European by mimicking a 1970s' Spanish holiday airport for customer care and speed of delivery. We don't bother trying to mimic their football teams, their fabulous red wine or even their food - no, we identify the one thing that irritated every single traveller throughout the whole of the 1970s and finessed it to an even lower standard of our very own!"

"If there was a direct Scottish translation for the phrase "mañana, mañana" it would be "we cannae be arsed right now" … Jesus …" he moaned.

"Don't worry" said Roops "It'll be here now. Even they can't lose it on such a short flight …" throwing in one last morsel of doubt into the head of the already irritated Jamie.

Evidence that human life does exist outside the corrugated gates comes in the shape of a large footprint on Jamie's bag as it finally trundles along the sad black belt, looking tired and dishevelled like a little tyke from a "Just William" comic strip, its demeanour that of the child who knows it's in deep trouble when it gets home.

The first touch of the bag immediately gives him a full weather report of outside - it was unusually cold and sodden implying that it had been held by the side of the tarmac just long enough for it to experience the harshness of the most inclement of the Scottish weather.

"Now we're ready to get home," said Jamie as he put his trolley case back in its familiar position, roughly three feet behind him.

"What's that noise?" said Roops as they walked to the Exit door.

"Aw shit" said Jamie as he realised it was one of his wheels clicking every couple of seconds as it slapped on the airport floor. "One of the wheels must have had its side flattened when it was hurled off the plane by a bloody baggage handler ... baggage mis-handlers they should be called ... Do you think I should I go and speak to someone? Get compensation?"

"I reckon you'll get laughed out of the place Jamie. Maybe just tough this one out eh? Let's get home now" reasoned Roops with a sense of weariness.

Jamie headed off to the tram stop, the flattened wheel on his bag clicking every couple of feet which made Roops laugh. He looked weary and the noise coming off his case just reinforced the view that he'd been through a bit of hell.

Roops headed off to the Pre-Booked taxi spot at the airport to collect his contract cab.

There was absolutely no way he would be getting a tram because as he'd said, it didn't cater for the masses. And, he reckoned, he'd given up enough over the last couple of days that the company could stretch to getting him a taxi to his front door.

And, in spite of his mood when he gets a taxi in the morning, the taxi journey home is actually quite a pleasant experience. Pleasant in a familiar type of way - it gives him a warm glow as he settles into the rear of the beautifully maintained Edinburgh taxi. Edinburgh taxi's are held to a notoriously strict and high standard by the local Taxi Inspector which means that when you step into them, it's like walking into a new furniture shop - a point that Roops never fails to make when in the back of a London cab.

Roops actually felt a lot of sympathy towards the taxi drivers who come into Edinburgh airport. He often felt that they get a pretty raw deal of things.

Throughout Edinburgh, taxis alongside buses, cyclists and emergency vehicles get special privileges to use Green Lanes and even certain roads. This is because they are generally more environmentally friendly and help to reduce the appalling congestion which curses Edinburgh's roads.

At Edinburgh airport however, taxis appear to be exploited. Unless you have a special contract with the airport, the taxis are exposed to the same £1 drop-off charge and the £3.90 pick-up charge as everyone else is. Whether the general public believe that the charge is fair or not is one thing - but for local businesses who are supporting the transport infrastructure, and the environment, it seemed harsh to Roops.

And of course, when a taxi driver isn't happy, nobody wins especially if you then have to spend 30 minutes with them, trapped in the back of their cabin.

Roops stepped into the rear of his cab. This particular one was white and had a garish tartan blanket laid across the back seat again extending the whole "Welcome To Scotland" bit for the unsuspecting tourists. It really just needed some shortbread to complete the whole experience.

But Roops didn't mind it actually. Sitting in the back of the taxi with an Edinburgh cabbie was to his mind, his first proper experience of being back home. With the familiar Edinburgh brogue spouting from the front of his cab, he felt firmly back on home turf.

"You been far off, mate?" came the voice from the front of the cab.

Roops looked himself up and down in a mock comedic gesture and looked over at his bag.

Here he was, sat on Braveheart's throne, wearing a smart business suit, a shirt with a cut-away collar and a Liberty tie which itself was knotted in a full Windsor. He had his highly polished brogues on and his favoured Mont Blanc cufflinks, his "luggage" consisted of one small bag with barely enough room for anything other than his work things and a small change of clothing.

There was absolutely nothing about him that implied he had been anywhere "far off". He just laughed to himself. This was a well worn routine for him but he positively embraced it.

It's remarkable he thought. Edinburgh cabbies seem to think that whoever they pick up from the airport has just returned from some far off land which has no internet access or even television with streaming 24 hour news channels - or certainly, if their conversation is anything to go by.

From here, there followed the formulaic routine from the taxi driver which always starts with a weather report of the last couple of days.

"Oh, you'll be glad to have been away mate. It's been raining up here. I mean, really raining with loads of flooding. The council need to sort out their potholes because that downpour just opened things up," he started telling Roops.

Now when Roops started travelling, it took him a bit of time to work out the real meaning behind all of this. Initially, he would think "Why is this guy telling me about weather that's already been? I'm more interested in the weather that's going to happen, over the next two days? And nowadays, I've got an app or a website that can tell me if it's really important to me?"

It was only after several episodes of this though that Roops started to get to the important aspect of this. The guy invariably wasn't telling you for your interest, he was actually giving you an insight to how crap his last two days had been - he was telling you the things that really mattered to him.

"I thought rain was good for you guys?" enquired Roops "Don't more people get taxis when it rains, even just for short journeys?"

"Aye, they do mate. But the golf course was flooded and we had to cancel our wee outing that we'd had planned …" came the response, the full truth beginning to unfold.

Taxi drivers live for the time they're not in their cabs and in Scotland, that invariably means "time on the golf course". Rain is not a good thing for this, although it's by no means disastrous. It usually takes a full scale monsoon with a blizzard thrown in for good measure to keep most of them off the course. But at least it was now clear why the driver decides you need to know about the weather you'd missed whilst you were away - he's really reliving whether or not he'd managed to get his quota of golf in for the week.

"If you don't mind mate, I'm going to go through Corstorphine tonight. There's murder roadworks on the bypass and I think someone's had an accident so we best avoid that area altogether. Why on earth they've decided to do roadworks at this time of year is beyond me. We've only just got over the roads being lifted for the trams and now they want to dig up another road over there. They don't always need to be using their shovels! Shovels are quite happy sitting in their sheds for a while you know. They're ridiculous this lot," he would say, completely oblivious to the fact that you'd actually only been away for a couple of days.

"Maybe it was because of the recent rain you mentioned and the potholes …?" ventured Roops.

Roops would reflect that their reports on the state of the roads was probably better aimed at someone who'd maybe been in prison for the last 15 years rather than someone who'd literally been away for what amounted to, in total, roughly 38 hours.

Then you get the local sports report. Roops was always astonished at how quickly the drivers were able to work out which side of the City you favoured in terms of local football teams but then again, maybe it was really obvious.

Here was Roops, sitting in his smart suit, hair neatly combed, with the ability to speak lucidly and in complete sentences, so for the taxi driver it was obvious that his passenger's team of choice sat in the west side of the city in the suburbs of Gorgie. You didn't have to be an avid watcher of CSI or Silent Witness to see the clues.

Roops had become adept though at gradually disengaging from the tête-à-tête with his driver and use the time to gradually reacclimatise with his surroundings. It was the first time in days that he'd had the opportunity to properly sit back, in something like his own space and just think. He would hear the familiar sounding accent from the front of the cab but without really listening to what it was saying. He would drift away, looking out of the windows taking in the sights that he grew up with.

His heart would pound that little bit faster, that little bit fuller as he swelled with pride as he took in the view of what he believed was not only the most wonderful city in Scotland, it was, Roops would eulogise, the most wonderful city in the UK, Europe and for him, the world.

Tonight was a beautiful evening in Edinburgh. The sun was beginning to set to the west behind Roops and his taxi, projecting a glorious orange hue over the city skyline. The route the driver was taking this evening, as a result of congestion and roadworks of course, was particularly poignant for Roops. In the distance, he could see Edinburgh Castle, enveloping its centuries old blanket of comfort over her City, as in the foreground Murrayfield Stadium, home to some of the country's most humiliating displays of rugby, pokes its head over the suburban houses on the west side of the city.

Memories of his childhood come flooding back and in particular, his mind would cast back to the familiar, but pungent smells coming from the numerous breweries fermenting their latest Eighty Shilling beers and India Pale Ales, sweeping across the skies. He remembered the conversations he'd have with his grandfather who would tell him of when these smells would mix with the smoke billowing out of the fireplaces in the many tenement buildings dotted around the city, giving the place its famous nickname, Auld Reekie.

Roops always took time to take in the view over to his right when he was on this route, to look over at the magnificent Pentland Hills which protected the city from the very worst of the incoming weather (which is a relative statement of course given this is Scotland). These hills had etched into them the artificial ski slope at Hillend crawling up their side like an enormous spider's web, the cause of many a broken thumb visiting the local A&E at the Royal Infirmary.

To his left, he could see the top of the various bridges spanning the Firth of Forth. The Road Bridge, which looks like a grey version of the Golden Gate bridge in San Francisco, and the new Queensferry Crossing side by side. Roops would muse on what they might be thinking as they posture alongside each other - the old and the new, the young and the old arguing, no doubt, about progress versus legacy.

But he could gaze for hours at the mother of them all - the original Forth Bridge. Roops could never stop himself from correcting the uninitiated who would insist on calling it the Forth Rail Bridge in an attempt to differentiate it from the old 1964 carbunkle which was the Road Bridge. If ever there was a structure, he would think, that never ever needed differentiating then it was the Forth Bridge. Quite simply, to his mind, it is the most beautiful man-made structure he had seen.

Of course, alongside its beauty, it also spawned the most enduring story of having a never ending paint job. Alas, even technology has caught up with that one and that truth has now become a myth.

"It's good to be home," Roops would think to himself. A sadness would come over him at this point, a strange knot in his stomach would emerge. He could never work out why but it always happened. It was as if he was about to be confronted in the family home by something that he hadn't seen coming, or that he was being dropped back into a storyline that he'd missed for two days unaware of the ongoing conversations as he would furiously try to get back up to speed with family life.

As his cab approached his house, he would often wonder whether this would be the day that the lampposts and the gates would be festooned in a sea of yellow ribbons with Tony Orlando booming from the windows. Maybe there would even be a balloon - "that would be quite nice" he would think.

But the reality was of course that he was to all intents and purposes just returning from his work. In one way, it's no different to what everyone else has had to do just from a bit further away. But to Roops, it was a million miles away and a million miles different.

And of course, he was stinking. Although he looked very smart, he had the stink of a few days of living out of a bag, his feet drenched from wearing the same shoes, his shirt sticking to his back, his skin with a sheen of sweat from his bad living, mixed with drying skin from the harsh wind he seemed to have constantly been walking into at every corner he turned.

His first priority when walking through the door was to shed this uniform which by now he hated with every bone in his body and disrespected even more. He could never remove it quickly enough, ripping the tie from his neck, unbuttoning his shirt and removing his trousers virtually all at the same time. All of this thrown with contempt into one pile on the floor before tipping out similarly stale smelling clothes from his overnight bag.

Before even engaging in any sort of conversation with his family, he just had one thought - the shower. This was his haven, the stinging heat of the water pounding against him washing away the dirt and grime built up - both physically and metaphorically - over days of misery in the City.

Roops would use this to wash away from his mind the memories and troubles of the last few days. This was his starting point to returning to be a proper loving family man. He would struggle against the misery that all of this would be starting again in just a few more days time.

"Is it all worth it?" he would ask himself. "Are you worth it? Why do you do it? Are you happy? Is this really what you aspired to be?".

Question after question would channel through his mind.

Questions which he could never really answer because ultimately their answer seemed irrelevant. How churlish, he would think, to even question this existence when he was so lucky to have everything around him.

People like Jamie would positively jump at the chance to have his life - how can he even begin to question it? He has a great way of life, is fortunate to see some amazing parts of London and experience things that others would need to pay a fortune for.

He has an incredible amount of freedom and trust placed in him and most importantly, he's genuinely good at what he does. He absolutely loves his job. He oozes enthusiasm for it.

But.

"Is this "the life" or is it just "my life"? he would ask himself. "Is this really fulfilling me in the way I want it to? I'm just not sure …" he would think. It gnawed away at him constantly.

"I wonder how my story will end."

Printed in Great Britain
by Amazon